Twayne's United States Authors Series

Sylvia E. Bowman, *Editor*

INDIANA UNIVERSITY

Mary McCarthy

MARY McCARTHY

by

Barbara McKenzie

Since 1937 and the appearance of Mary McCarthy as a drama critic in *Partisan Review*, the writing of Miss McCarthy has attracted significant attention. *Cast a Cold Eye*, the title of a collection of her essays, is characteristic of its author. In turn, the cold glances that she has cast in her autobiographical sketches, critical essays, short stories, novels, and travel-art histories have provoked in her readers a variety of glances —ranging from the warmly admiring to the chillingly hostile. Invariably, reaction to the writing of Miss McCarthy has a temperature.

This study seeks to examine the contribution of Mary McCarthy by analyzing the major concepts that provide her subject matter and the "method" that gives shape to these concepts. Emphasis on Miss McCarthy's concern for exposing the *actual* behind the *apparent* has led to an investigation of her use of satire and irony in works from *The Company She Keeps* (1942) to *The Group* (1963).

It is the author's intention in this appraisal to capture the essence of the "irreducible and always recognizable" voice of Mary McCarthy.

MARY McCARTHY

By BARBARA McKENZIE

Drew University

Twayne Publishers, Inc.   ::   New York

MANUFACTURED IN THE UNITED STATES OF AMERICA BY
UNITED PRINTING SERVICES, INC.
NEW HAVEN, CONN.

To
LESLIE AND EUPHEMIA MCKENZIE

Preface

L *IFE* describes her as the "lady with a switchblade." *Gent* finds her dangerous but not in herself responsible: "A time produces its artists and so we must all take the blame for Mary McCarthy." Mary McCarthy is being talked about, and not altogether in the most laudatory terms. But Miss McCarthy has *been* talked about ever since 1934 and her book-reviewing days for *The Nation,* primarily because of the incisiveness of her characterization of the twentieth-century intellectual and his hangers-on.

Miss McCarthy has said, concerning characterization, that she tries to find the key that works the pérson "both in real life and in the fiction." This critical study is an attempt to find the key that "works" the fiction and essays of Mary McCarthy—another way of saying the person of their author; for Miss McCarthy is a very personal writer in a very public way. The chapters that follow explain this apparent contradiction.

The emphasis in the first two chapters is biographical. The first describes Mary McCarthy's life from the outside—using as material the "facts" found in *Who's Who,* book reviews, and so on; and the second presents her life from the inside as she explains her childhood and adolescent years in *Memories of a Catholic Girlhood.* The third chapter concerns Miss McCarthy as a drama critic and essayist. Most of the essays in *On the Contrary* are not related to literature, but those that are explain Miss McCarthy as a writer; she knows herself well and is, perhaps, her own best critic. The fourth chapter considers the short stories (a number of which can be labeled more properly as "essays") that are collected in *The Company She Keeps* and *Cast a Cold Eye.*

The essay and short story collections reveal Mary McCarthy's ability to see in the specific, the generic—and in the generic, the idiosyncratic. This ability is the gift of the satirist, and the next two chapters discuss the satirical vision that gives shape to *The Oasis, The Groves of Academe, A Charmed Life,* and *The Group.*

Important to this analysis of Mary McCarthy as a novelist is a discussion of her method and esthetic theories. *Venice Observed* and *The Stones of Florence,* the travel-art books, are the subject of Chapter Seven. The final chapter appraises the contribution of Mary McCarthy to the literature of our time.

One of Mary McCarthy's critical concerns is the author's voice—"the irreducible and always recognizable" voice. And it is precisely this voice that is lost in a critical analysis such as this one. Lost, perhaps, but not entirely so, or at least this is my hope. For it is Mary McCarthy's voice—"irreducible and always recognizable"—that makes her one of the most important and gifted and uncomfortable writers in America today.

BARBARA McKENZIE

Drew University

Acknowledgments

I am grateful to Professor Clark Emery of the University of Miami and to Mrs. Jacqueline Berke of Drew University for guidance in the composition of this book.

I would like to make further acknowledgments to the following:

To Harcourt, Brace & World, Inc. for permission to quote from *The Company She Keeps*, copyright, 1939, 1941, 1942, by Mary McCarthy; *Cast a Cold Eye*, copyright, 1944, 1946, 1947, 1948, 1949, 1950, by Mary McCarthy; *The Groves of Academe*, copyright, 1951, 1952, by Mary McCarthy; *A Charmed Life*, copyright, 1954, 1955, by Mary McCarthy; *Memories of a Catholic Girlhood*, copyright, 1946, 1948, 1951, 1952, 1953, 1955, 1957, by Mary McCarthy; *The Stones of Florence*, copyright, 1959, by Mary McCarthy; *The Group*, copyright, 1954, 1963, by Mary McCarthy.

To Reynal & Company, Inc. for permission to quote from *Venice Observed*, copyright, 1956, by Mary McCarthy.

To Signet Books for permission to quote from *The Oasis*, copyright, 1949, by Mary McCarthy, first Signet printing September, 1963.

To Farrar, Straus & Co., Inc., the Noonday Press division, for permission to quote from *On the Contrary: Articles of Belief, 1946-1961*, copyright, 1946, 1947, 1949, 1950, 1951, 1952, 1953, 1954, 1955, 1958, 1959, 1960, 1961, by Mary McCarthy, copyright, 1951, by The Curtis Publishing Company; *Mary McCarthy's Theatre Chronicles, 1937-1962*, copyright, 1937, 1938, 1940, 1943, 1944, 1945, 1946, 1947, 1948, 1949, 1954, 1955, 1956, 1957, 1958, 1959, 1961, 1962, 1963, by Mary McCarthy; *A View of My Own: Essays in Literature and Society*, copyright, 1951, 1953, 1954, 1955, 1956, 1958, 1959, 1960, 1961, 1962, by Elizabeth Hardwick.

To *The Paris Review* for permission to quote from "The Art of Fiction XXVII," an interview with Mary McCarthy, Elisabeth Niebuhr as interviewer, which first appeared in the Winter-Spring, 1962, issue.

To *Esquire Magazine* for permission to quote from "Mary McCarthyism" by Brock Brower, which appeared in the July, 1962, issue, copyright © by Esquire, Inc.

To Doubleday & Company, Inc., for permission to quote from "The Novels of Mary McCarthy" by John Chamberlain, from the book, *The Creative Present* by Nona Balakian and Charles Simmons. Copyright © 1963 by Nona Balakian and Charles Simmons.

Contents

Chronology

1912 Mary McCarthy born in Seattle, Washington, June 21, 1912.

1918 Move to Minneapolis; death of parents.

1923 Return to Seattle.

1929 Graduation from Annie Wright Seminary.

1933 Graduation, B.A., from Vassar College; marriage to Harold Johnsrud.

1936 Separation and divorce from Harold Johnsrud.

1936- Position with Covici Friede, publishers.
1937

1937- Drama Editor, *Partisan Review.*
1938

1938 Marriage to Edmund Wilson; birth of Reuel Wilson.

1942 Publication of *The Company She Keeps.*

1945 Separation from Edmund Wilson.

1945- Instructor in Literature, Bard College.
1946

1946 Divorce from Edmund Wilson; marriage to Bowden Broadwater.

1948 Instructor of English, Sarah Lawrence College.

1949 Publication of *The Oasis*; recipient *Horizon* prize.

1949- Guggenheim fellow.
1950

1950 Publication of *Cast a Cold Eye.*

1952 Publication of *The Groves of Academe.*

1955 Publication of *A Charmed Life.*

1956 Publication of *Sights and Spectacles;* publication of *Venice Observed.*

1957 Publication of *Memories of a Catholic Girlhood.*

1959 Publication of *The Stones of Florence.*

1959- Guggenheim fellow.
1960

1961 Publication of *On the Contrary;* divorce from Bowden Broadwater; marriage to James Raymond West.

1963 Publication of *Mary McCarthy's Theatre Chronicles, 1937-1962;* publication of *The Group.*

Mary McCarthy

CHAPTER 1

The Fact in Biography

ALTHOUGH Mary McCarthy acknowledges in the preface to *The Company She Keeps* (1942) that "the home address of the self, like that of the soul, is not to be found in the book," the undiscoverable object of the search undertaken by Margaret Sargent, the autobiographical heroine of this collection of short stories, is "the ordinary, indispensable self" that somehow has been misplaced.[1] Almost twenty years later, when questioned about this work and these statements, Miss McCarthy replied: "I was very young then. I think I'm really not interested in the quest for the self any more. . . . What you feel when you're older, I think, is that . . . you really must *make* the self. . . . I don't mean in the sense of making a mask, a Yeatsian mask. But you finally begin in some sense to make and to choose the self you want."[2]

Obviously, the facts of biography also fall short of disclosing the "home address of the self" of Mary McCarthy. The details that define and add particularity lie in the aggregate of the essays and fiction that comprise the totality of the published work of Miss McCarthy and beyond that, forever elusive, in the person of their author. But the objectively rendered facts of biography can serve to indicate the direction where the "self" resides.

I *Family Influences*

Mary Therese McCarthy was born in Seattle, Washington, on June 21, 1912, the first of four children. Her mother, Therese Preston McCarthy, was the daughter of Harold Preston, a well-known Seattle lawyer of New England ancestry, and of Augusta Morganstern Preston, "a lively Jewish beauty from San Francisco."[3] Her father, Roy Winfield McCarthy, came from Minneapolis where his father, J. H. McCarthy, had made a sizeable fortune in the grain-elevator business. Both families had objected on medical and religious grounds to the marriage. At the time of her wedding, Therese Preston had not yet converted to Catholicism. Roy McCarthy, ten years her senior, suffered from chronic heart disease. But parental opposition went unheeded.

Roy McCarthy was a winsome man, carefree and recklessly extravagant, in spite of ill health. Fond of tricks and surprises, he could turn the slightest occasion or action into a treat. The Seattle years were filled for his young daughter Mary with "a succession of birthday cakes and ice-cream molds, a glorious May basket . . . , a hyacinth plant, parties with grab bags and fish ponds. . . ."[4] Although a lawyer, he seldom practiced law since an allowance of eight or nine hundred dollars a month from his father was sufficient to provide the basic income for the family. Tiring eventually, however, of the improvidence of their son, the elder McCarthys decided that he and his family should move to Minneapolis where his expenditures could be supervised more closely.

Disregarding the many warnings to avoid public places, Roy McCarthy and his family left Seattle at the height of the influenza epidemic of 1918. A week later, Therese Preston McCarthy died at the age of twenty-nine in Minneapolis; her husband survived his wife by one day. The pleasure-filled years of young childhood ended abruptly for Mary McCarthy who, along with her three younger brothers, became one of "poor Roy's children." The recollection of the years spent in Minneapolis and of her removal in 1923 (under the aegis of Harold Preston) to Seattle, where she lived until 1929 under the guardianship of her maternal grandparents, forms the basis of *Memories of a Catholic Girlhood* (1957).

In Minneapolis, she and her brothers were placed in the care of their grandmother's sister, Margaret, and Myers Shriver, Margaret's newly acquired husband. Apparently too uncertain of herself and her unfamiliar role as wife to counter her husband's wishes, Margaret allowed Myers, a boorish and cruel man, to dominate the household and to mete out his own brand of injustice. During this time, although J. H. McCarthy provided generously for his grandchildren (Mary McCarthy reports that from 1918 to 1923 he spent $41,700 for their support), he chose to ignore that Myers and Margaret were failing to provide a home commensurate with the sums of money allocated to them. Miss McCarthy recounts the bleakness of these years and the curious indifference of her grandparents in "Yonder Peasant, Who Is He?" and in "A Tin Butterfly," two essays collected in *Memories of a Catholic Girlhood.*

But another abrupt transition took place in 1923 when Harold Preston intervened. Only Sheridan, the youngest child, was permitted to stay with Myers and Margaret. Kevin and Preston entered a Catholic boarding school, and Mary returned to Seattle with her grandfather. Gradually, the five unpleasant Minneapolis years, like those of the earlier Seattle period, were dimmed by the immediacy of a contrary setting. Like the years of very early childhood, however, the interval spent with Myers and Margaret could never be erased totally. Miss McCarthy's fiction, as well as her non-fiction, attests to the influences of childhood and to the tenaciousness of memory.

At the age of eleven, Mary McCarthy entered the seventh grade of Forest Ridge Convent in Seattle. As a boarding student, she spent weekends and holidays with her grandparents in their spacious, peaceful home. Margaret had limited her ward's reading material to either the instructional or the Catholic-drenched (Myers seldom read and therefore had remained indifferent), but in Harold Preston's library, Mary McCarthy discovered sets of Dickens, Frank Stockton, Tolstoy, Bret Harte, and Bulwer-Lytton. In addition, the latest volumes from the circulating library were accessible: Ben Hecht, Carl Van Vechten, Mencken, Cabell, and Aldous Huxley. Once again substitutions had occurred. This time the fair-mindedness and trust of the Prestons had replaced the injustice and suspicion of Myers and Margaret. Lacking still, however, were exuberance, affection, and permissiveness—important qualities associated with memories of her parents.

After spending the ninth grade at a public high school in Seattle, she entered the Annie Wright Seminary, in Tacoma, the following year. There she remained until 1929, when she was graduated as the top student in her class. While a junior at the seminary, she "discovered" Latin: "Latin came to me very fluently, probably because of my Catholic training, but I felt as if I had known it in another incarnation. Hence writing with a Latinate turn, compressed, analytic, and yet having a certain extravagance or oratorical flourish sounded in my ears like a natural, spoken language."[5] During the summer of 1929, she enrolled in acting classes at the Cornish School in Seattle; and in the fall of that year, still hopeful of becoming an actress despite having found the drama school a disappointment, she entered Vassar College and a more "public" phase of her life.

II *Vassar College*

Mary McCarthy found Vassar to her liking. Approximately twenty years after her undergraduate days, she revisited the campus and described what she saw (and, more than most persons, Miss McCarthy has a habit of seeing what she wants to see) in an essay entitled "The Vassar Girl" (1951). This essay is interesting in that the differences Miss McCarthy noted between the Vassar of the early 1950's and that of the 1930's establish rather clearly the basic likes and dislikes that inform much of her other writing. On the post-World War II campus, she found that "the idea of excellence, the zest for adventure, the fastidiousness of mind and humanistic breadth of feeling" that had characterized Vassar life when she was a student were missing.[6] In her eyes, the girls appeared settled and complacent: "Their plans are made—one will be a doctor; one will work for the UN; another will take up journalism. There is none of the conflict and indecision that harried us in the thirties; they have decided to help the world, but not to change or destroy it" (204).

In addition, she observed that the campus-dominated student life, with its many extracurricular activities, allowed little time for "solitude and self-questioning" (208). The college, she declared, had become "a miniature welfare state," furnishing social direction as well as education, emotional guidance, and pleasure (208). "To the returning alumna whose college years were both more snobbish and sectarian, on the one hand, and more Bohemian, rebellious, and lyrical, on the other, the administrative cast, so to speak, of the present Vassar mold is both disquieting and praiseworthy" (209-10).

In all probability, the present-day Vassar student would protest the unfairness of these sweeping generalizations and point out that an abundance of extracurricular activities does not preclude discrimination and that self-styled "aesthetes" still exist, just as they did twenty years earlier. But, to Miss McCarthy, the reduction in both expectation and achievement that she noticed on the part of the later day Vassar girl represents an obvious and unfortunate change. In part, this essay is a protest against the fake democratization that takes as its assumption the equal distribution of intelligence, ability, and opportunity.

Perhaps nowhere in her writing does she make her attitude toward this kind of "equality" more explicit than in the foreword to *Memories of a Catholic Girlhood* when she describes St. Stephen's, the school she attended in Minneapolis: "There was no idea of equality in the parochial school, and such an idea would have been abhorrent to me, if it had existed; equality, a sort of brutal cutting down to size, was what I was treated to at home. Equality was a species of unfairness which the good sisters of St. Joseph would not have tolerated." Accordingly, "snobbish" and "sectarian," as used in "The Vassar Girl," depend less on values associated with money and family (the very rich, in her writing, are usually described as insensitive and insulated because of their wealth) than with attitudes and actions that stem from high expectations and high standards.

In June of 1933, Mary McCarthy was graduated from Vassar College full, as she reports, of Juvenal, Martial, Catullus, Shakespeare, Nashe, and Greene. She was joyous to be leaving college precisely because she had loved it and, like her classmates, was anxious to enter the larger world beyond the college gates. "Vassar," she explains, "had inspired us with the notion that the wide, wide world was our oyster" (200). A scant few years later, a census revealed that "the average Vassar graduate had two-plus children and was married to a Republican lawyer" (200). But such was not to be the fate of Mary McCarthy. One week after graduation, she married Harold Johnsrud, an actor whom she had met in Seattle the summer she had studied acting at the Cornish School, and settled in New York City. The essay "My Confession" (1953) tells part of the story of this marriage and of the political movements with which she came in contact from 1933 until 1938.

III *New York City in the 1930's*

Although Mary McCarthy's professional activities (she had begun to write short book reviews for *The New Republic* and *The
Nation*) were introducing her to left-wing politics, neither she
nor Johnsrud were serious politically. Not until the fall of 1936,
after her divorce, did she become embroiled in the political factions of the Left. By accident (because of the company she kept
and a chance remark at a party), she found herself on the "Committee for the Defense of Leon Trotsky." She perversely stayed
on the committee, despite her ignorance of its aims, because of
"advice" from Communist Party members to sever her relations
with the Trotsky partisans and because of a natural inclination to
champion the underdog. At the time, she did not foresee how this
allegiance would change her life. "I had no notion that I was now
an anti-Communist, where before I had been either indifferent
or pro-Communist."[7]

All the important decisions in her life, she admits, have shared
this accidental nature: "The 'great' decisions—those I can look
back on pensively and say, 'That was a turning-point'—have been
made without my awareness. Too late to do anything about it,
I discover that I have chosen. And this is particularly striking
when the choice has been political or historic" (76). This curiously passive acceptance of events has its counterpart in the sexual
passivity of the Mary McCarthy heroine who, more often than
not, finds herself in bed with a man for whom she appears to
have no strong desire.

During the 1930's, as well as continuing to review for *The
Nation* and *The New Republic*, she worked at Covici Friede, a
left-wing publishing house no longer in existence. Then, as a result of her alliance with the Trotsky committee and the inter-
locking circles of the leftist movement, she became acquainted
with Philip Rahv who, along with William Phillips, was attempting to revive *Partisan Review* as an anti-Stalinist magazine.[8] Not
surprisingly, the first issue of the renovated *Partisan Review,*
appearing late in 1937, listed among its editors Mary McCarthy.
Although anti-Stalinist, none of the editors (with the exception
of Dwight Macdonald and he but for a short time) was an active
Trotskyite; experience with the Communist Party had made each
cautious of direct political ties. Mary McCarthy, along with Rahv

and Phillips, admired Trotsky, however, as an exponent of the Marxist doctrine and agreed with most of his criticism of the Soviet regime. Trotsky, she wrote, "possessed those intellectual traits of wit, lucidity and indignation which I regarded, and still regard, as a touchstone."[9] Nonetheless, to the *Partisan Review* "boys," Mary McCarthy remained absolutely bourgeois. She recalls them saying to her sternly, " 'You're really a throwback. You're really a Twenties figure.' "[10] Because of their disbelief in the depth of her political commitment and because they considered the theater of no consequence, they assigned her the theater column. Her drama reviews are collected in *Sights and Spectacles: 1937-1956* (expanded in 1963 and published under the title *Mary McCarthy's Theatre Chronicles*).

IV *The Writing of Fiction*

In 1938, she married Edmund Wilson who encouraged her to attempt writing fiction. She recalls: "After we'd been married about a week, he said, 'I think you have a talent for writing fiction.' And he put me in a little room. He didn't literally lock the door, but he said, 'Stay in there!' And I did. I just sat down, and it just came. It was the first story I had ever written, really: the first story in *The Company She Keeps*."[11] Robert Penn Warren published this story, "Cruel and Barbarous Treatment," in the *Southern Review* (Vol. IV [Spring, 1939]). And, to Mary McCarthy's "great surprise," she found herself writing fiction. Although no longer an editor of *Partisan Review,* she continued to contribute the theater column.

From 1945 to 1946 (she and Wilson had separated in 1945), she taught at Bard College, an experience she enjoyed because she likes studying. In 1946, she divorced Wilson, "the impediment apparently being that 'my mind was so totally different from Edmund's,' " and married Bowden Broadwater.[12] This marriage, which lasted until 1961, has been described as " 'a rest for Mary' " and as "a quiet reading period" (66). But Mary McCarthy did not "rest" during those fifteen years from the labor of writing. In 1949, *Horizon* published *The Oasis*, for which she received its literary prize. The year 1950 saw the publication of *Cast a Cold Eye*. The list of her published works increased quickly: *The Groves of Academe* (1952), *A Charmed Life* (1955), *Sights and*

Spectacles and *Venice Observed* (1956), *Memories of a Catholic Girlhood* (1957), and *The Stones of Florence* (1959).

Then, in 1961, after her divorce from Bowden Broadwater, she married James Raymond West, a United States diplomat. That same year *On the Contrary,* a collection of essays, was published. In 1963, *Theatre Chronicles* appeared. The year 1963 marked also the publication of *The Group,* a novel which, as a result of its appearance on the best-seller lists, has brought the name, if not the purpose, of Mary McCarthy to a wider reading public. For her purpose is tied in, of course, with her "method" or, to put this another way, her "style." And her style, as she admits, rests on exaggeration and hence on distortion. *The Group* is not a realistic account of Vassar College graduates, although it pretends to be—as any good mock-chronicle should. But such comments irrefutably lead away from the outlines of biography into the "self" of the author or at least into as much of that self as the shape and substance of the published works reveal.

V *Paradoxes and Mirroring*

Like any work of art, the writing of Mary McCarthy sustains a life independent of its creator. Yet a highly personal quality in her writing insists on a recognition of the close relation between art and life. Brock Brower protests mildly against calling Mary McCarthy an *-ism;* but the tag, he states, has a certain appropriateness: "She has given such a detailed record of her affairs, marriages, political leanings, and other follies—and, incidentally, arrogated to her own use so many of the trials she has caused others—that she really has become her own central idea" (65). As "her own central idea," however, she mirrors in her writing the peculiar predicament of other American women who, like her, have been ensnared by the modernity they champion.

James Agee, in a letter to Father Flye dated August 18, 1932, describes the prevailing spiritual tone of the early 1930's as "the darkest and saddest in centuries."[13] Science and "scientific-quasi-ethical thought" have worked evil as well as good by bringing

something almost like destruction into love. To say nothing of the *foul* results of *feminism.* It may resolve for the women of the next generation or two but this generation suffers hell for it:

trying to live an uneasy egocentricity they can't sustain, unable
to reconcile it with love, which they could, and ruined in love
by the grinding of old conventions to which they've been
trained, against new conventions which they honestly feel compelled to live by. . . .[14]

Mary McCarthy writes often about the kind of woman Agee so
bleakly describes. In a sense, her writing presents a composite
Portrait of the Intellectual as a Woman. The woman who has sat
for the portrait is often unappealing: affected, discontented,
argumentative, and striving. Only by studying the portrait more
closely does the reader discern in the subject both an inner uncertainty and an evanescent inner joy. As a consequence, the
recognition of these two qualities allows him to *accept* the
heroine and even to laugh at her plight—as she herself does.
Mary McCarthy is, indeed, one of the most comic writers in
America. And because humor demands distance, the comic element helps to endow the singular writing of Mary McCarthy
with larger meaning by affording this distance.

The essays and fiction of Mary McCarthy present, too, the
paradox of education. In "Odd Man In" (1959), she says:
"Education and sensitivity are supposed, by those who have
them, to constitute some sort of guarantee or safeguard; that, in
fact, they do not is the terrible and banal discovery of the non-
hero."[15] Such a recognition is not limited, however, to the non-
heroes of O'Neill and Genêt, the principal dramatists she discusses in this essay; for the "heroines" of Miss McCarthy's fiction
likewise make this "terrible and banal discovery." Education,
they come to realize, is not a carte blanche to a "useful" and
"meaningful" life. In turn, this paradox explains another premise
that underlies much of the writing of Mary McCarthy. If man
cannot learn in any meaningful sense, then education is powerless to protect him against the hypocrisy and emptiness of contemporary existence. *The Groves of Academe* dramatizes, in
particular, this assumption. Jocelyn College is sadly flawed because its practitioners—both students and teachers—are sadly inadequate; they resist change. Education, Miss McCarthy implies
in this novel and elsewhere, does not touch man at the center of
his being; consequently, it fails to affect beneficently or otherwise his moral choices. Like money or family or environment,

education as portrayed in the fiction of Mary McCarthy remains an external.

Much lauded as a novel of ideas, *The Groves of Academe* turns, nonetheless, on its characters; for, despite a tendency to see characters in terms of externals (part and parcel of her "method"), Miss McCarthy's strength as a novelist and short-story writer rests to a great degree on her ability to create characters that are believable and capable of giving life to the ideas that bulwark the fictional piece. That many of her characters are defined by externals and remain unaffected by time is what makes them real and what forever designates them to the realm of the comic. Or so Miss McCarthy maintains in her essay "Characters in Fiction" (1961).

Like many-sided mirrors, the essays of Mary McCarthy help to explain her fiction; and the fiction, in turn, dramatizes the premises of many of the essays. *Memories of a Catholic Girlhood* becomes interesting, therefore, not only as a series of personal memoirs that give dimension to the outlines of biography but as a collection of essays that set down certain themes and attitudes that also sustain her fiction. In this manner, the very "privateness" of autobiography helps to explain much of what becomes public in the other writing of an author who is, consistently and interestingly, her own central idea.

CHAPTER 2

Childhood and the Distance of Time

THE FIRST ESSAY in *Memories of a Catholic Girlhood*—"Yonder Peasant, Who Is He?"—achieves unity through the commanding presence of Lizzie Sheridan McCarthy, the paternal grandmother of Mary McCarthy. Concerning this "ugly" and "severe old woman," Miss McCarthy remarks in "Yonder Peasant": "Luckily, I am writing a memoir and not a work of fiction, and therefore I do not have to account for my grandmother's unpleasing character and look for the Oedipal fixation or the traumatic experience which would give her that clinical authenticity that is nowadays so desirable in portraiture."[1] "To the Reader," a foreword to the collection as a whole, contains, however, this apparently contradictory statement: "Many a time, in the course of doing these memoirs, I have wished that I were writing fiction. The temptation to invent has been very strong, particularly where recollection is hazy and I remember the substance of an event but not the details . . ." (3-4). This kind of inconsistency is characteristic of *Memoirs of a Catholic Girlhood* which is not straight reporting. Miss McCarthy freely admits that certain portions—the conversations in particular—are invented: "Quotation marks indicate that a conversation to this general effect took place, but I do not vouch for the exact words or the exact order of the speeches" (4).

In addition to the prefatory "To the Reader," each of the essays[2] (with the exception of the last) is followed by an epilogue which both amplifies the preceding material and attempts to sort fact from fancy. These afterwords and the preface were added by Miss McCarthy when she collected the autobiographical sketches that had been appearing in periodicals, principally *The New Yorker*, since the 1940's and arranged them for publication in the present form. The reaction of critics to the insertion of these addenda has customary variety. Some resent any intrusion into the world their fancy has wrought from the reading of the initial essays. Katherine Hoskins criticizes the epilogues as "superficial."[3] The reviewer in *The Times Literary Supplement* (November 29, 1957) finds the "second thoughts and factual corrections . . . unhelpful." Other critics, however, consider the reflections in keeping with the theme of self-scrutiny and articulation that informs the work. *Memories of a Catholic Girlhood,* Victor Lange observes, "does not pretend to offer us either barren facts or spurious truth, but hints as to the infinite inconclusiveness of insight and judgment."[4] In autobiography, as Elizabeth Hardwick has noted, the conflict between self-exposure and self-justification gives the form its dramatic tension.[5] Certainly this observation holds true of *Memories of a Catholic Girlhood.* But the occasional contradictions that occur, as well as the backtracking evidenced in some of the "second thoughts," contribute also to the dramatic tension that binds the separate essays into a cohesive whole.

In the interview that appeared in *The Paris Review* (Winter-Spring, 1962), Mary McCarthy explained that she enjoyed doing *Venice Observed* and *The Stones of Florence* because she was writing in her own voice. Conversely, in her novels and short stories she has engaged in a masquerade, feigning such alien consciousnesses as that of Henry Mulcahy in *The Groves of Academe* and submerging her voice in those of her characters. In portions of *Memories of a Catholic Girlhood,* she likewise has used a kind of narrative mimicry, for the distance of time necessitated a looking back and a consequent re-creating of a former, half-forgotten self. Thus Mary McCarthy was faced with the curious task of mimicking herself at the age of nine or twelve or fifteen in order to make that alien and yet familiar self believable to the reader. The result of this practice is a few over-rhetorical flourishes that contrast sharply with the precise and wittily severe prose characteristic of *Memories* as a whole. Despite the shifts in tone they occasion, these purple passages do succeed, however, in conveying admirably the vivid imagination and suggestibility of Miss McCarthy as a child.

I *Themes within the Framework of Autobiography*

In addition to being unified by the dramatic tension created by
the exigencies of the autobiographical form and by the rehashing
that goes on in the epilogues, *Memories of a Catholic Girlhood*
achieves coherence through certain persistent themes which, as
noted previously, also "sustain" the fiction of Mary McCarthy.
But the events and people and ideologies that shaped her world
as a child have done more than provide the substance of autobiography or the impulse to write short stories and novels. Unquestionably, the experiences that she dramatizes in *Memories*
determined the kind of writer she would become. Specifically,
the events of childhood gave rise to the satiric vision that dom-
inates Miss McCarthy's fiction. ". . . Hypocrisy is the greatest
single source of satiric material," maintains Leonard Feinberg in
his recent study on satire.[6] Mary McCarthy very early became
acquainted with hypocrisy.

A major theme in *Memories* is Catholicism or, more precisely,
the effects of Catholicism. Miss McCarthy admits that she finds
assessing the influence of her Catholic heritage difficult because
it "consists of two distinct strains." On the one hand was the
Catholicism that she had learned from her mother and from the
nuns and parish priests in Minneapolis, "a religion of beauty and
goodness, however imperfectly realized" (21). The ugly church
and St. Stephen's—the parochial school run by the sisters of St.
Joseph—provided, as she recalls, her "only aesthetic outlet, in
the words of the Mass and the litanies and the old Latin hymns,
in the Easter lilies around the altar, rosaries, ornamented prayer
books, votive lamps, holy cards stamped in gold and decorated
with flower wreaths and a saint's picture" (18).

On the other hand was the Catholicism practiced by Lizzie
Sheridan McCarthy and by Myers and Margaret, "a sour, baleful
doctrine in which old hates and rancors had been stewing for
generations, with ignorance proudly stirring the pot" (21). Miss
McCarthy characterizes the piety of her paternal grandmother
as "an act of war against the Protestant ascendancy" (33). Although lacking in the Christian virtues of humility and charity,
Lizzie Sheridan McCarthy was nonetheless unshakeably complacent about the rightfulness of her beliefs and actions. This
kind of unjustifiable smugness has caused Miss McCarthy to

remark that religion—particularly Catholicism and the sense of privilege that it fosters, "the notion that not everyone is lucky enough to be a Catholic"—is morally dangerous in that it opens the gate to the deadly sins of pride, anger, and sloth. Thus, religion becomes good only "for good people." For others, like her Minneapolis relatives, religion "seems to bring out some of the worst traits in human nature and to lend them a sort of sanctification" (22).

Admittedly, this is a harsh conclusion, but the evidence supports such a judgment. Neither compassionate nor generous, Lizzie Sheridan McCarthy could remain indifferent to the reality of the children's appearance—the darned and patched clothing, the raw hands and scarecrow arms, their silence and "elderly faces"—because her husband's checkbook assured her that the children were being well provided for and because her Catholicism granted her a superiority and rectitude that made questioning unnecessary. She had bought an immunity in much the same manner that her brand of Catholicism allowed her to "buy" absolution through the act of confession. Concerning the ideology of a related religious practice, Miss McCarthy has written, "I never really liked the doctrine of Indulgences—the notion that you could say five Hail Marys and knock off a year in Purgatory. This seemed to me to belong to my grandmother McCarthy's kind of Catholicism" (26).

As a child, Mary McCarthy recalls, she was aware of the discrepancy between the unpleasant and unesthetic house superintended by Myers and Margaret and the comfortable and overtly gracious home of her grandparents. Neither she nor her brothers, however, attempted to complain to their grandfather except silently, by running away. On these occasions, the truant child, after appearing unannounced at the home of the McCarthys, would be allowed

> to sleep in the sewing room, a bleak, shabby, utilitarian rectangle, more office than bedroom, more attic than office, that played to the hierarchy of chambers the role of a poor relation. . . . Thin white spreads, of the kind used in hospitals and charity institutions, and naked blinds at the windows reminded us of our orphaned condition and of the ephemeral character of our visit; there was nothing here to encourage us to consider this our home. (29)

In regard to J. H. McCarthy, she explains, "We were too poor, spiritually speaking, to question his generosity, to ask why he allowed us to live in oppressed chill and deprivation at a long arm's length from himself . . ." (31). In fact, when Harold Preston intervened, after being apprised at last of the unhappy situation, his indignation surprised the children: "We thought it only natural that grandparents should know and do nothing, for did not God in the mansions of Heaven look down upon human suffering and allow it to take its course?" (46).

In the epilogue to "Yonder Peasant," Miss McCarthy has acknowledged that as a child she viewed her grandmother with more favor than the portrait in *Memories* suggests. At that time, Lizzie Sheridan McCarthy seemed to her "a tremendous figure," awesome and worldly, whose faults appeared admirable qualities. Even as an adult, the epilogue to "A Tin Butterfly" reveals, Miss McCarthy finds a partial excuse for her grandparents on the grounds that if they had recognized the truth they would have had to separate the children, "either putting us in schools to board (for which we were really too young) or distributing us among the family (which my aunts and uncles would probably have resisted) or letting the Protestants get some of us" (53).

With her maternal grandparents in Seattle, however, Mary McCarthy doubtless became aware of the possibility of actions corresponding to words and of her right to share the graciousness that in Minneapolis she had been allowed to admire only from afar. In short, the fairness of the Prestons must have exposed the hypocrisy of her paternal grandparents who, despite evidence of their muted awareness of the actual circumstances, took no steps to improve the situation and were content instead to receive approbation from the community for their "extraordinary munificence" toward "poor Roy's children." Accepting praise for acting in a manner distinctly unpraiseworthy is, of course, a form of hypocrisy. Early, it seems, the contrasts in Mary McCarthy's childhood dramatized for her the vulgarity and cruelty of pretension and the injustices that stem from a sense of complacency and superiority. At least, such are the forms of hypocrisy that much of her fiction seeks to satirize.

A second major theme that runs through *Memories* concerns the contrast between outward appearance and internal reality. Like the recognition of hypocrisy (with which it is closely allied), this awareness has also affected Miss McCarthy's method as a writer. In "To the Reader," she recounts the first instance of her acknowledgment of the need to sustain outwardly acceptable behavior at the expense of inner truth. On the morning of her first Communion, she unthinkingly took a drink of water. To take Communion after having broken the fast would be, she knew, to accept the Holy Sacrament in a state of mortal sin. Not to take Communion, however, would incur her guardians' anger, the sisters' disapproval, and her classmates' disappointment. "So it came about: I received my first Communion in a state of outward holiness and inward horror, believing I was damned . . ." (20).

Subsequent moral crises in her life, Miss McCarthy affirms, have followed "the pattern of this struggle over the first Communion; I have battled, usually without avail, against a temptation to do something which only I knew was bad, being swept on by a need to preserve outward appearances and to live up to other people's expectations of me" (20-21). On that Communion morning, when she supposed herself damned, Miss McCarthy admits that in actuality she was fated "to a repetition or endless re-enactment of that conflict between excited scruples and inertia of will" (21).

This recognition of the difference between external and inner reality, or between the way things *seem* and the way things *are,* provides the disposition and subject matter of irony. The fiction (and for that matter, most of the nonfiction) of Mary McCarthy employs irony, which is to say that the form of her writing depends not only upon a need to expose and to ridicule, the objective of satire, but upon a deep and consistent awareness of the contradictions of human experience. In her fiction, Miss McCarthy often abandons the exaggeration and distortion of satire in favor of a level-headed, precisely worded presentation of the incongruities of what it is to be human. Irony, in other words, is seldom absent from Mary McCarthy's writing even though it does, at times, get lost amid the less profound trappings of satire. Resting on an awareness of the multiple levels and purposes of life, the ironical vision is, by definition, the result of a mature but resigned wisdom that counteracts the moments of self-indulgent contrariness that have made critics charge Mary McCarthy with precocity.

The awareness of the discrepancy between the way things seem and the way things are and the resultant need to behave so as to preserve appearances introduces a third major theme—the necessity of compromise. This theme, which Miss McCarthy links with the acceptance of maturity, figures most prominently in her essays that deal primarily with education. For purposes of further analysis, the essays in *Memories* can be grouped into two distinct categories: those dealing with the McCarthy and Preston families, the stress being on character; and those concerning her life as a boarding-school student in Seattle and Tacoma, the stress being on education and an ever deepening awareness of the need to compromise.

II *Grandparents and Guardians*

The family essays, those forming the first group, comprise "Yonder Peasant, Who Is He?", "A Tin Butterfly," "The Black-guard," and "Ask Me No Questions." "Yonder Peasant," as Mary McCarthy has acknowledged, differs from the others in that it is primarily "an angry indictment of privilege for its treatment of the underprivileged, a single, breathless, voluble speech on the subject of human indifference." Miss McCarthy describes this essay as "a kind of allegory or broad social satire on the theme of wealth and poverty" (49). "Yonder Peasant" is more than an allegory, however, and her grandparents are more than "specimens of unfeeling behavior." Lizzie Sheridan McCarthy stands fully realizable as a person who is relentless in her sectarian righteousness and resplendent in her dubious majesty. Much of the effectiveness of this essay depends on the sharp contrast between the comfortable home of the J. H. McCarthys and the bleakness of the "dingy house two blocks distant" where the McCarthy children lived in relation to their grandparents as peasant to feudal lord. Like the inhuman feudal barons described in history books, the elder McCarthys made no effort to inquire about the "where and what" of their grandchildren's dwelling.

The second essay, "A Tin Butterfly," is principally a character study of Myers Shriver, the husband of Miss McCarthy's great-aunt Margaret; and, partially, in the concluding paragraph and in the epilogue, it is an acknowledgment of the fallibility of memory. In addition, this essay dramatizes another major theme found in the writing of Miss McCarthy—the importance of having

a history. Myers was baffling precisely because he appeared to
have neither trade nor history. "He came from Elkhart, Indiana,
but beyond this fact nobody seemed to know anything about
him . . ." (59). In "To the Reader," Miss McCarthy acknowledges
that part of the initial impulse that caused her to undertake these
autobiographical sketches was the need to establish her own
family history: "As orphans, my brother Kevin and I have a burning interest in our past, which we try to reconstruct together, like
two amateur archaeologists, falling on any new scrap of evidence,
trying to fit it in, questioning our relations, belaboring our own
memories" (6). Paradoxically, she admits that the difficulties in
this task of reconstruction have turned out to be an incentive.
The importance of having a history also has an application to the
fiction of Miss McCarthy, for the history that she "invents" for her
characters—in addition to their taste in visual objects or their
actions—helps to explain them to the reader. Also, to the extent
that a person's history makes him "intelligible" by "explaining"
him, so Mary McCarthy's *Memories of a Catholic Girlhood*, by
giving her a history, represents an effort on her part to achieve
greater self-understanding.

The apparent dissociation of Myers from his past has caused
Mary McCarthy to characterize him as "the perfect type of rootless municipalized man who finds his pleasures in the handouts
or overflow of an industrial civilization" (60). The amusements
Myers enjoyed consisted chiefly of parades commemorative of
national holidays or commercial interests, public parks without
grass, band concerts, sky-writing, department-store demonstrations, free samples, cemeteries, soldiers' monuments, and street-
car rides. A rare excursion with the McCarthy children to a
public park furnished the crisis that provides the "plot" for "A
Tin Butterfly." During the course of the outing, Sheridan (the
youngest child) found a tin butterfly in a box of Cracker Jack
that Myers had bought for him. When, a week or so later, the
butterfly (a worthless ornament, but much prized by Sheridan
and his brothers) disappeared mysteriously and then reappeared
just as mysteriously by Mary McCarthy's place at the dinner
table, the guilt fell on her. Despite her protestations of innocence,
she was severely beaten.

The concluding paragraph describes a family reunion that took
place about seven years later. At that time, Preston told his sister

"that on the famous night of the butterfly, he had seen Uncle Myers steal into the dining room from the den and lift the tablecloth, with the tin butterfly in his hand" (80). The epilogue challenges this interpretation, for at a still later date, neither Kevin nor Preston could remember Preston's having assigned the guilt to Myers, as Mary McCarthy had described him as doing. Thus the guilt of Myers remains as undetermined as his history. And memory, in this instance, has proved inadequate to repair the "chain of recollection" that had been broken by the death of Roy and Therese McCarthy.

The third essay, "The Blackguard," concerns Miss McCarthy's maternal grandfather, Harold Preston. The setting is the Forest Ridge Convent in Seattle at a time when Mary McCarthy, a child of eleven, was in the seventh grade. Part of the charm of the convent-school education stemmed from the drama of the "dark-horse doctrine of salvation" and the resultant admiration of the sisters (Ladies of the Sacred Heart) for the great sinners and atheists of history: "Like all truly intellectual women, these were in spirit romantic desperadoes. . . . Marlowe, Baudelaire—above all, Byron—glowed like terrible stars above their literature courses. . . . Even M. Voltaire enjoyed a left-handed popularity" (93). These infatuations were shared by their pupils. Accordingly, when Madame Barclay, the prefect of studies and the most severe of the teachers, accused Mary McCarthy of being "just like Lord Byron, brilliant but unsound," the young girl was highly flattered and waited impatiently to tell her grandfather. Far from sharing his granddaughter's enthusiasm, Harold Preston construed the tribute as an insult and telephoned the Mother Superior, angrily questioning the right of one of her sisters "to associate his innocent granddaughter with that degenerate blackguard, Byron." At the next class meeting, Madame Barclay retracted her statement publicly and announced that Mary McCarthy was "neither brilliant, loose-living, nor unsound" (96).

In addition to using this incident to contrast the rock-bound sternness of Harold Preston with the romantic indulgences and greater liberality of imagination of the sisters, Miss McCarthy reintroduces the theme of Catholicism. This time, however, the effects of Catholicism, although neither "practical" nor conventionally moral, are nonetheless beneficial. The convent school fostered an atmosphere in which the imagination could flourish and, in addition, created in Mary McCarthy an understanding of the necessity of preserving a historical perspective—an awareness evidently lacking in the character of Harold Preston.

In "Ask Me No Questions," the last essay of the collection, the central figure is Augusta Morganstern Preston. As an adult, Mary McCarthy had come to associate what was mysterious about the Preston family with this vain, secretive woman. As in "A Tin Butterfly," the importance of having a history acts as a controlling theme.

Almost all that Mary McCarthy knew about her grandmother was that she had come to Seattle while still in her teens from San Francisco where her father had been a "broker" (of what sort Miss McCarthy never determined). Prior to that, he had left Europe (from what country Mary McCarthy does not know) in 1848, lived in Pennsylvania one year, and then traveled to California during the gold rush of 1849. This, basically, comprised her grandmother's history. Undemonstrative and inflexible, Augusta Preston had sealed off her inner life as securely as she closed her bedroom door at twelve o'clock each day in order to prepare for her afternoon visit to downtown Seattle.

Although Mary McCarthy never knew her grandmother's feelings about her Jewish heritage, she did in later years gain insight into Augusta Preston's closed nature. Augusta Preston had two sisters, the oldest of whom was Eva, "a typical wealthy widow of Jewish high society." Her Jewishness, Miss McCarthy observes, appeared only to make her unconscious of values and personages divergent from her own. Rosie, the other sister, was quite different. To Rosie, active in the community life of Seattle —particularly the musical events of the Metropolitan Theatre, "being Jewish was simply a matter of religion" (207). Because she did not recognize barriers, she crossed them naturally. On the occasion of Rosie's sudden death, Mary McCarthy happened to be visiting her grandmother. At that time, Augusta Preston's wild and extravagant grief caused Miss McCarthy to realize that her grandmother "had never really cared for anyone but her sister; that was her secret." As she attempted to comfort the hysterical woman, she became aware "that some sort of revelation had taken place—of the nature of Jewish family feeling, possibly. . . . Of one thing I was certain: my grandmother was more different from the rest of us than I could ever have conceived" (243).

Although Harold and Augusta Preston were kind to their granddaughter, they were also distant. Mary McCarthy had entered their lives, but seemingly she had not affected the outward motions of their conduct. She recalls, "When I think of our house now, the strongest memory that comes back to me is of shut doors and silence. . . . I remember those summer mornings during school vacations. . . . The silence was profound. Every member of the family, except me, was taciturn—the cook and the gardener, too" (229). Inhospitable to callers, Augusta Preston prevented effectively the intrusion of "outsiders"; and, just as effectively, she blocked all questions that concerned matters of personal history.

III   *Education and the Growth of Awareness*

"C'est le Premier Pas Qui Coûte," "Names," "The Figures in the Clock," and "Yellowstone Park" concern education or, more precisely, the effects of education. Two corollary themes unify this group of essays. The first has to do with compromise and receives its motivation from the differences that exist between appearance and reality and the consequent need to preserve appearances in order to live up to the expectations of others. The second theme centers on a concept of maturity that involves a heightened recognition of what is possible, a leveling of expectation—in short, a state of being that allows compromise to flourish.

The "plot" of "C'est le Premier Pas Qui Coûte" centers around a deliberate bid for attention on the part of Mary McCarthy. As a seventh-grader and a "new" student at Forest Ridge Convent, she had been denied admittance to the clique of older girls that "ruled" the school despite such momentary fame as that occasioned by Madame Barclay's tribute. Accordingly, when Mary McCarthy returned the next fall as an eighth grader and a full-time boarder, she was resolved to attract notice, despite a growing awareness that she could not seek prominence without appearing somewhat ridiculous. After considering various devices to win the spotlight, she chose, as the most dramatic, to lose her faith and then to regain it publicly during the three days of a forthcoming retreat. Ironically, by pretending to doubt, she soon discovered that she no longer really believed certain of the teachings of the Church. Interviews with the Mother Superior, the old chaplain from a neighboring Jesuit college, and a young Jesuit missionary who was leading the retreat only strengthened her disbelief instead of restoring her faith.

In the meantime, however, her "ruse" had proved effective: "Little queens who had never noticed my existence gathered round me at recess and put me whispered questions, for we were not supposed to talk during the retreat. The coincidence of the holy fervor of the retreat with my unsanctified state heightened the sense of the prodigious" (121). But by the third day, when she had still not regained her faith, "a sort of uneasiness settled down over the convent. It was clear to everyone, including me, that I would *have* to get my faith back to put an end to this terrible uncertainty" (122). As "a public duty," therefore, Mary McCarthy pretended to be converted the following morning when she knelt at the altar railing to receive the host—this action was "the cost of the first step." Also, in enacting this fraud, she was repeating the situation of her first Communion by once again existing in a state of "outward holiness and inward horror," buoyed by the need to conform to other persons' expectations of her and aware in so doing of the discrepancy between appearance and reality.

The coyness apparent in parts of this essay results from an attempt by Miss McCarthy to reproduce syntactically and idiomatically the romantic, ego-involved imaginings that characterized her at the age of twelve. For example, before she had decided upon losing her faith, she had debated about the advisability of eloping with the Swedish baron who was their music master. She writes: "I grew faint when my laced shoe encountered his spatted Oxford on the loud pedal. Examples of child marriages among the feudal nobility crowded through my head, as if to encourage the Baron, but at length I had to bow to the force of American custom and face it: he probably thought I was too young" (111). Later, as well as likening herself to the young Jesus when she was considering the dangers involved in losing her faith, she reasoned: "He who hesitates is lost; *qui ne risque rien n'a rien,* observed the devil, lapsing into French, as is his wont" (112). Despite the preciousness of such passages, mimicry of this sort does reproduce authentically the high-flown fantasies of childhood.

The next essay, "Names," is based on an earlier essay, "C.Y.E.," first published as "a short story" in *Mademoiselle* (April, 1944) and later included in *Cast a Cold Eye* (1950). Mary McCarthy states that when she put "C.Y.E." in *Cast a Cold Eye,* she was unaware of her dislike for this early autobiographical sketch. By the time that she was putting together *Memories of a Catholic Girlhood,* she admits candidly, "I simply couldn't stand it, and when I was reading the book in proof, I decided to tear it out, to reduce it to a tiny tiny incident. As it stood, it was just impossible, much too rhetorical."[7]

In the earlier essay, as in "Names," the action results principally from a nickname—C.Y.E.—assigned to Miss McCarthy while a student at Forest Ridge Convent. Because the unwritten code of the convent prevented her from learning the meaning of the name, she made wild attempts to guess. Her imagination suggested both the outlandish, such as "Catch Your Elbow" or "Cheat Your End," and the sensible and humiliating "Clean Your Ears." Believing that the name had a profound meaning, she became convinced of a sense of an irremediable and immanent spiritual taint that separated her from the older convent girls whom she admired. And she knew that even in the parochial school in Minneapolis where she had been popular, she had felt a wrongness, "a kind of miserable effluvium of the spirit that the ordinary sieves of report cards and weekly confessions had been powerless to catch."[8] As she made plans to leave the convent at the end of that academic year, she resolved: ". . . once I was out of the convent, I would never, never, never again let anybody see what I was like. That, I felt, had been my mistake" (127).

The essay at this point switches to the present, as a suggestion as to what the letters C.Y.E. stand for comes into her consciousness: Clever Young Egg. Cheered by this thought, she longs to embrace the past, shorn of the feelings of self-loathing occasioned by the hated nickname. The past, of course, cannot be recaptured. As she remembers the students at Forest Ridge Convent, she sees herself as she was then, a pale, plain girl sitting in the front row of a study hall. She greets her "with a touch of disdain for her rawness, her guileless ambition. . . . I hate her, for she is my natural victim, and it is I who have given her the name, the shameful, inscrutable name that she will never, sleepless in her bed at night, be able to puzzle out" (128). The "natural victim" is the unsophisticated and "over-weening" and "over-intense" self that Mary McCarthy long ago, in the eighth grade, decided not to "let anybody see." Paradoxically, as an adult, Miss McCarthy is eager to expose and explain this despised and un-charming self to whom she now stands as enemy.

In "Names," only a few paragraphs concern the acquisition of the nickname C.Y.E. This essay emphasizes instead Mary Mc-Carthy's fear, as an eighth grader, of appearing ridiculous to others. The assumption that she "could not seek prominence without attracting laughter" can be explained in terms of her Catholic training. As a child she had felt her "religion very in-tensely and longed to serve God better than anyone else" (19). By the time of "C'est le Premier Pas Qui Coûte," however, the focus of her emotions had changed considerably. "Curiously enough, for the first time, seeing what I had wrought, I had a sense of obligation to others and not to my own soul or to God, which was a proof in itself that I had lost God, for our chief obligation in life was supposed to be to please Him" (122). Traditionally, the Church teaches that the only pride man should have in himself is that which comes through God. By replacing God with "others," Miss McCarthy's concern for preserving ap-pearances had become sinful. Thus a sense of guilt was at least partially responsible for her growing fear of appearing ridiculous. That Mary McCarthy as an adult remembers vividly this adoles-cent fear (and, in a way, the autobiographical heroine of *The Company She Keeps* evinces a similar self-consciousness and ap-prehensiveness about the reactions of others) is further evidence that, even after many years, she is aware still of an all-too-human vanity and an all-too-vain humanism.

In addition to offering a somewhat different set of circum-stances surrounding the acquisition of the nickname C.Y.E., "Names" gains wider scope by including a general discussion of the importance of names to the Catholic and of the exotic names of many of the older convent girls. In turn, these observations allow Miss McCarthy to discuss briefly the cosmopolitan nature of Seattle and to contrast the foreignness of the Pacific North-west with the parochialism that characterized her existence in Minneapolis.

The re-introduction of the by now familiar theme of compromise broadens the scope of "Names" still further. In this instance, a cut on her leg had stained the bottom sheet of her bed
with blood. When she requested a clean sheet, the nun on
dormitory duty assumed immediately that the girl had begun to
menstruate and dispensed a cloth girdle and a flannel sanitary
napkin. An interview with the Mother Superior ensued. The more
Mary McCarthy tried to protest that the blood had issued from a
scratch on her leg, the more Madame MacIllvra believed that the
girl was frightened and embarrassed by what had supposedly
happened. At length, Mary McCarthy had to give in and "pretend
to have become a woman, just as, not long before, I had to pretend to get my faith back—for the sake of peace" (134).

She was burdened with this sense of fraud when she was
assigned her nickname, C.Y.E. The convent school, she was
forced to admit, did not agree with her.

> The oddest part was all that pretending. There I was, a walk-
> ing mass of lies, pretending to be a Catholic and going to con-
> fession while really I had lost my faith, and pretending to have
> monthly periods by cutting myself with nail scissors; yet all
> this had come about without my volition and even contrary to
> it. But the basest pretense I was driven to was the acceptance of
> the nickname. (136)

Only through failing to answer to this name during her first
weeks at the public high school the following year did she finally
lose some of the "sense of wrongness" associated with C.Y.E.

The next essay, "The Figures in the Clock," takes place during
Mary McCarthy's senior year at the Annie Wright Seminary, an
Episcopalian school in Tacoma. In addition to dramatizing again
a situation in which Miss McCarthy found herself yielding to a
half-truth in order to satisfy the expectations of others, this essay
re-introduces, through Miss Harriet Gowrie, the important part
that having a "history" plays in human relationships. Another
central concern of "The Figures in the Clock" is found in two
personages from Roman history—Caesar and Catiline—and to the
absolutes of justice and lawlessness that they symbolize. The
predilections not only of Miss McCarthy but also of Miss Gowrie,
the Latin teacher, alternated between the fair-mindedness of
Caesar and the corruptness of Catiline, "like the two little

wooden weather figures in a German clock, one of which steps out as the other swings back into the works, in response to atmospheric pressures" (160).

The substance of this essay concerns an analysis of Catiline and Caesar and Miss McCarthy's identification with these historical personages. To dramatize her relationship to Catiline, she uses the device of a Latin club play in which she took the role of Catiline: "adulterer, extortioner, profligate, bankrupt, assassin, suspected wife-killer, broken-down patrician, democrat, demagogue, thug" (144). Her admiration for Caesar had developed when she had begun tutoring with Miss Gowrie: "The sensation was utterly confounding. All my previous crushes had been products of my will, constructs of my personal convention, or projections of myself, the way Catiline was. This came from without and seized me; there was nothing that could have warned me that Caesar would be like *this*" (154). It was at this time that Mary McCarthy realized that there was "another" self hidden behind her Catilinarian poses, a self sufficiently mature to admire the justice and detachment of the *Commentaries*—those qualities in Caesar that made him the opposite of Catiline.

The incident that dramatizes the theme of equivocation and compromise involves the enigmatic Miss Gowrie, a dour Highland Scotswoman. Whether in actuality the Latin teacher played an important part is problematic. (In the epilogue Miss McCarthy admits that she rearranged some of the actual events so as to make a good story, a temptation difficult to overcome: "If you are in the habit of writing fiction, one does it almost automatically.") As a junior, Mary McCarthy had "discovered" Miss Gowrie and had tried, with a group of classmates, to show their fellow students that underneath her stoicism the Latin teacher was warm and pleasure-loving. Their efforts at uncovering the "real" Harriet Gowrie were, however, to no avail. Miss McCarthy writes: "So far as we could determine, she had no private life or history and consisted totally of national attributes (thrift, humorless hard work, porridge-eating, and tea-drinking) . . ." (149). To the end, Miss Gowrie remained the only instructor who attempted to enforce the seminary rules, many of which, as Miss McCarthy acknowledges, existed for "artistic reasons"—for form's sake.

When late one night in June, Miss Gowrie caught her star pupil sneaking through a gymnasium window, she reported the girl to the administration. In the interview with the principal that followed, Miss McCarthy realized that she was not being questioned directly as to why she had left the school property; and she knew too that if she told the truth—that she had gone out to meet a boy—the principal would be forced to expel her, despite the fact that graduation was imminent. On the other hand, a partial truth would allow her to graduate. ". . . I was the top student in my class, and the school, I perceived, was counting on me to do it credit in my college boards." In addition, she knew that by lying she could vindicate Miss Gowrie and her misguided super-surveillance. Miss McCarthy writes: "A sense of power and Caesarlike magnanimity filled me. I was going to equivocate, not for selfish reasons but in the interest of the community, like a grown-up responsible person" (162). Believing that a "lie was a favor" the principal was asking of her, she explained that she had left the school building to smoke which, since she had smoked, was partially true. The principal accepted this confession and the compromise worked.

Again, as in the instance of her first Communion or of her pretended conversion at the convent school, Miss McCarthy had acted in order to preserve appearances and to conform to the expectation of others. Or so she thought, for here again is evidence of the self-exposure and self-justification characteristic of autobiography. A different construction could be put on the situations that Miss McCarthy has described. In this incident, quite possibly the truth would not have deterred Mary McCarthy from graduating. Public avowals to the contrary, administrators have been known to close their eyes to infractions of greater seriousness than that perpetrated by Miss McCarthy, especially if committed by a senior student a week before graduation. Likewise, did she really have to pretend while she was at the convent to get her faith back or did she only *think* that she must pretend to be converted? There can be no answers to such questions. These instances, however, point to the unintentional self-exposure associated with the personal memoir.

In the next essay, "Yellowstone Park," which appeared first in *Harper's Bazaar* (November, 1955), Mary McCarthy is a year and a half younger than she was at the time of "The Figures in the Clock." Although the setting is non-academic, this essay describes an experience that caused Mary McCarthy to learn and continues to depict the necessity and effects of pretense. In addition, more than any other essay in the collection, "Yellowstone Park" concerns a confrontation with the meaning of maturity, an awareness that involves compromise in the largest sense of the word. In this essay, the lesson Mary McCarthy learns concerns a recognition of the limitations of adulthood, an understanding that rests in part from being able to comprehend the complexities of a situation.

In order to get Harold Preston to approve of her spending part of the summer at the home of Ruth and Betty Bent in Medicine Springs, Montana, Miss McCarthy used a tour of Yellowstone Park as a lure to convince her grandfather of the educational benefits to be derived from such a vacation, Actually, nothing of the sort had been planned: the Bent sisters had promised their visitor an endless round of parties and dates. To qualify for this social life, Mary McCarthy had posed to her friends at the seminary "as a practiced siren." Her whole life, she admits, was a lie, "for if I was wilder than my family knew, I was far tamer than my friends could imagine, and with them, too, as with my family, I was constantly making up stories . . ." (173).

Contrary to Mary McCarthy's expectations, Medicine Springs was not a fashionable spa but a small, flat, yellowish town; and far from an abundance of handsome, eligible young men, the entire male population, with one exception, was married. Most of the essay is a hilarious account of the "social" life of Medicine Spring as arranged by the Bent girls. In "Yellowstone Park," a strong element of the comic (untouched by a streak of pathos, for the situation is more of the author's own making) asserts itself. As in much of her other writing, Miss McCarthy utilizes for the purposes of creating humor the failure of actuality—in this instance Medicine Springs—to live up to expectation. This basic device accounts for most of the satire in *The Oasis* and in "The Man in the Brooks Brothers Shirt," a short story that appears in *The Company She Keeps.*

Since the only single man in town "belonged" to Ruth Bent, and a young man soon to be divorced (which in Medicine Springs made him practically single) had been claimed by Betty, their guest was awarded Bob Berdan, a man of twenty-five whose wife was away visiting relatives. The first night set the pattern for the following evenings. After setting out across the prairie in three separate cars, the party would stop so that a bottle of moonshine could be passed around, after which the caravan would start again, only to stop a short while later for another round of moonshine, and so on—far into the night and the prairie. On that first evening, not wanting to admit that she had never tasted hard liquor, Miss McCarthy accepted the bottle but found that the whiskey gagged her. Repeated tries proved no more effective until she discovered that by holding her nose, she could swallow a mouthful. Finally, becoming ashamed of having to hold her nose, she discovered still another method: "I could take a gulp and hold it in my mouth and work it down gradually, when no one was looking, a few drops at a time. This prevented me from talking for long periods. Bob Berdan sang, and I rode along tight-lipped beside him, with a mouth full of unswallowed moonshine . . ." (181).

The account of Mary McCarthy's attempts to master the social life at Medicine Falls is comic also because of the incongruity of participant and setting and because of the stubborn and mechanical repetitions of her actions. Although she could not learn to drink the moonshine, as she admits, she refused to stop trying—a situation that resulted in the parade of cars having to halt "for me to throw up by the roadside. As soon as I had done so, the bottle would be passed again. When I was conscious, I was frequently speechless, owing to the fact that there was a gulp of moonshine in my mouth that I had not yet been able to swallow; it would sometimes take ten minutes to work it down" (184).

Concerning Bob Berdan, she writes that, although she was not aware of it at the time, she regarded him, like other adults, as "circumscribed and finite and yet encumbered, like all the rest of them, with a mysterious burden of feeling. In the back of my mind, I had a child's certainty that I was moving, going somewhere, while the grownups around me were standing still" (184-85). On the train back to Seattle, she experienced still another situation that gave her insight into adulthood. Bothered by her conscience, she sought to improve her knowledge of Yellowstone Park by talking with a group of tourists "fresh out of Yellowstone" who had boarded the train. Although they treated her as an "equal," they did not have, in her estimation, the necessary "grasp of detail" that would allow her to put together a narrative suitable for the ears of Harold Preston.

Accordingly, when a fatherly conductor warned his young passenger of the immorality of her traveling companions, she forsook their company, not because she was shocked, but because, if she continued to talk to the foursome, the conductor "would see that he had been duped in me. And I felt too old and weary to explain why I was not shocked." The dilemma in which she found herself, although again she did not comprehend its larger significance at the time, was "the trap of adult life, in which you are held, wriggling, powerless to act because you can see both sides. On that occasion, as generally in the future, I compromised" (189). In this instance her compromise consisted of talking to the foursome when the conductor was not looking and abruptly terminating the conversation when he was in sight. In Seattle, she reports, the treasures and serenity of the house allowed her to think that the improbable could occur within the confines of the familiar and to forget the bleakness of adult reality.

IV   *Reaction of the Critics to* Memories of a Catholic Girlhood

One detractor has termed *Memories of a Catholic Girlhood* the "Number One Cry-Baby Book of the Year" and has characterized Mary McCarthy as the "Boswell of her own ego."[9] Pointing out that to live joyfully one must love something, he concludes his "review" in this fashion: "Unable to find room in her heart for love, that empty, brittle heart has been unable to feed her emotions and intellect. She is left alone—floundering around on the hook of her own ego. That is, precisely, why she wants to resign from the human race. She writes well—but oh, with what an emptiness."[10] Discounting the absurdity that Mary McCarthy "wants to resign from the human race," what this reviewer fails to consider is that Miss McCarthy writes not from an abject despair but from a sense of disappointment in man and his institutions—a disillusionment caused by the discrepancy between expectancy and actuality or between high and noble ideals and their working out in the practicality of the every day. These are the recognitions that account for the emphasis on compromise and on the dull defeat of honesty. The theological philosopher may wish Mary McCarthy to have put her faith and love into a being larger than man, into a Creator or Divine Principle. But had she done so, that would have been another story and a different childhood. Another reviewer has questioned the use of "Catholic" in the title, since those essays subsequent to "Names" take place after she has left the Sacred Heart convent.[11] This criticism discounts the pervasiveness of the influence of Catholicism. Undisputedly, the Catholicity of her girlhood caused her to perceive her surroundings in a particular way and later to attempt to define that perception through autobiography.

Not so dominant, of course, is the theme of Jewishness. Although Augusta Morganstern Preston is the subject of only one essay, she affects, somehow, the work as a whole as in actuality she affected the life of her granddaughter. In "Ask Me No Questions," Mary McCarthy writes: "I myself had a curious attitude, I now realize, in which the crudest anti-Semitism ('Ikey-Mose-Abie,' I used to chant, under my breath, to myself in the convent) mingled with infatuation and with genuine tolerance and detachment" (211). As an adult, her attitude toward Jews evinces a fascination and tolerance similar in many respects to the feelings she assigned to her childhood self—as is apparent in much of her other writing, most particularly in "Artists in Uniform," an essay included in *On the Contrary.*

Critics have made much ado over Mary McCarthy's honesty in *Memories of a Catholic Girlhood.* And without doubt, *Memories* is an honest book—or as truthful as it can be. For, in all probability, no autobiography can be completely honest. The distance of time and the intense subjectivity demanded by the form prevent absolute truthfulness. Also, as the sketches in *Memories* indicate, Miss McCarthy in real life has had to struggle to be as truthful as she would like, a struggle heightened by a recognition of expediency and the accompanying subjugation of the "whole" truth. These contradictory awarenesses help to explain both her preoccupation with honesty—in herself and in others—and her intense admiration of honesty where she finds it. In the essays and in the drama reviews of *On the Contrary* and *Theatre Chronicles,* this personal ideal becomes objectified as a critical criterion to judge man and his activities.

CHAPTER 3

All Things Mortal

DURING THE TIME they were courting, Edmund Wilson once told Mary McCarthy, " 'You don't so much review a play as draw up a crushing brief against it.' "[1] Brock Brower notes, adding to Wilson's criticism, "The same could be said for all things mortal—bad writing, weak principle, political error, moral or mental lapse, the pandering of modern communications, or just the rather shaggy beast in men—that have fallen under her basilisk eye."[2] The reputation of "our First Lady of Letters" (as Norman Mailer dubs Miss McCarthy) rests, without question, as solidly on her critical writing as on her fiction. And perhaps she will be best remembered as a critic, for, in a sense, she may be accused of having written little else but criticism, so much are her short stories and novels mockingly and cleverly explanatory.

Mary McCarthy began reviewing books for *The Nation* and *The New Republic* soon after her graduation from Vassar College and her marriage to Harold Johnsrud in June, 1933. Most of these reviews concern books that have not "lasted." Like the early theater criticism that appears in *Partisan Review* from 1937 to 1945, they are interesting chiefly as bits of social history. But, like the theater criticism, they evince the author's short temper with bad writing and untruthfulness. Their contrariness soon attracted notice.

When *The Nation* in the fall of 1935 wanted "a large-scale attack on critics and book-reviewers, chiefly those in the *Herald Tribune*, the *Times* and the *Saturday Review*, and so on," Mary McCarthy and Margaret Marshall, then assistant literary editor, were assigned the task. Miss McCarthy explains: "I had been doing some rather harsh reviews, so they chose me as the person to do this." She and Miss Marshall divided the work, each doing separate pieces. "That series," Miss McCarthy continues, "was a great sensation at the time, and it made people very mad."[3] Small wonder. Appearing in the initial article and providing a thesis statement for the five installments is this turned-about paraphrase of T. S. Eliot: "Criticism in America during the past ten years has on the whole worked for the misunderstanding of works of art and the debasement of taste" (October 23, 1935).

All manner of critics came under fire—the "anti-intellectuals" (represented by Burton Rascoe, Carl Van Doren, and Isabel Paterson); the leading lights of the *Saturday Review of Literature* (Henry Seidel Canby, Christopher Morley, and William Rose Benét); the editor of the New York *Times Book Review* (J. Donald Adams); the Marxist critics of the *New Masses* (Kyle Crichton and Robert Briffault); and the "literary salesmen" of the New York daily newspapers (John Chamberlain, Lewis Gannet, Harry Hansen, and William Soskin). Criticism is best, Miss McCarthy and Miss Marshall reasoned, where it is farthest removed from publishers' advertising. By omitting other relevant considerations, this assumption leads irrevocably to the conclusion that the best criticism occurs in *The Nation* and *The New Republic* since these magazines, like the quarterlies, are not the pawns of advertisers.

This kind of hack work is not particularly honest. Neither are some of the early *Partisan Review* drama columns. As noted in Chapter I, the other editors accepted Miss McCarthy on the staff reluctantly because she was not a Marxist. But she was "the girl friend of one of the 'boys,' who had issued a ukase" on her behalf and by that time had "a minute 'name'" as well.[4] Acting on the conviction that the triviality of the contemporary theater would render any bourgeois lapses insignificant, the "boys" assigned her the "Theatre Chronicle."

The column had its idiosyncrasies, caused chiefly by the continuous attack of prevailing attitudes to which *Partisan Review* was dedicated. "Aesthetic puritanism, of which we were rampant examples and which, I believe, is absolutely necessary in America, has, like all puritanism, a tendency to hypocrisy—based on a denial of one's own natural tastes and instincts" (xii-xiii). Miss McCarthy recalls her uneasiness when she found herself liking *Our Town* by Thornton Wilder and being "almost" afraid to praise the play and thereby run the risk that the other editors would conclude that she was starting "to sell out" (xiii). Other peculiarities of the column—such as reviews of plays that had closed months earlier or gaps in the chronicle occasioned by Miss McCarthy's absence from the city—resulted from the lack of indebtedness of *Partisan Review* to theater managers for complimentary tickets and from the condition that most of the readers were not theatergoers.

The early reviews contain many Marxist terms and labels used, Miss McCarthy admits, "to tell the reader, in his own words, why he would agree with me . . ." (xiv). By the end of World War II, however, the reviews depend very little on the vocabulary of Marxism. Miss McCarthy has since declared that she finds the pedantic, condescending tone of the early reviews objectionable, but she has let them stand "in the interest of the record and because I think anyone who could write so foolishly owes a debt to society that cannot be cancelled out by the mere process of getting older" (vii). But, she says plainly, "I really hated the kind of theatre the regular critics liked or at any rate treated respectfully" (xiii).

I *As a Drama Critic*

Approximately seven months prior to the publication of the first "Theatre Chronicle," the May 8 and May 15, 1937, issues of *The Nation* included an article in two parts titled "Our Actors and the Critics." In this article, Miss McCarthy contends that drama criticism in America is purblind to acting because the American theater reviewer is unable to distinguish between manuscript and acting and between acting and direction. This failure has resulted in the critic resorting to such imprecise and catch-all terms as "brilliant," "sincere," and "moving" on the rare occasions that he does attempt to define the qualities he admires in certain actors. As Miss McCarthy points out, apprehending an actor's performance involves a variety of considerations. The critic must understand not only the actor's role but his role in relation to the play and the method or design chosen by the actor to convey his view of the role. The New York drama reviewers, she summarizes, are too frightened and lazy to have engaged in this kind of criticism.

The bias in this article hints at what is particularly successful in Mary McCarthy's own drama criticism. She does pay attention to actors and acting and to the details of production: sets, lights, make-up, costumes. She is aware of stage conventions and of innovations that defy these conventions. Only in the later essays that concern the contribution of a particular dramatist, such as Ibsen or Shaw, is the concentration chiefly on manuscript. But curiously enough, Roger Beckett, in a review of *Sights and Spectacles,* claims that, whether Mary McCarthy is watching Shakespeare or Ogden Nash, she sees only ideas: "The play itself is never the thing for her. The wonderful machinery going on before her eyes never itself delights her. Toward the stuff and substance of the theatre—the lights, the scenery, the faces, gestures, voices, make-up, costumes—the whole apparatus of make-believe on a stage, she is almost entirely oblivious."[5] Nothing could be more untrue. Miss McCarthy has a good eye for details and a tape-recorder memory. These attributes work to her advantage in everything she writes. Also she *knows* something about the history of the theater and about acting. At Vassar College, she had majored in Elizabethan literature and had taken part in several plays. Only near the end of her senior year did she abandon plans for an acting career: "I started to write instead, which did not interest me nearly so much, chiefly because it came easier."[6]

"Theatre Chronicle" proved a success. "People liked it, the editors decided. It was 'something a little different'" (x). What is different about the drama criticism of Mary McCarthy has to do with standards that have involved looking inward as well as outward—inward to a personally held concept of honesty which becomes a yardstick to judge the writing and performance of others; outward to what she terms articulate theater, represented by the works of such playwrights as Molière, Shaw, Chekhov, Turgenev, Ibsen, Montherlant, Strindberg, O'Casey, Hauptmann, Brecht, and Genêt. Opposed to these dramatists is Tennessee Williams or Arthur Miller whose writing, she finds, strikes a false note and for whom excuses are continually being invented, "as though he were some wretched pupil bringing a note from his parent: 'Please excuse Tennessee or Arthur or Clifford; he has a writing difficulty'" (xvii). The term "good theatre," she argues, is imprecise because it manages to dodge the center of pertinent dramatic criticism. What does it mean? she asks. "'Strong' situations? Masochistic grovelling? Sexual torture? Is

Sophocles 'good theatre'? Is Shakespeare? Apparently not, for the term is always used defensively, to justify a kind of shoddiness, which is held to be excusable for the stage" (xvi-xvii).

Another characteristic of Mary McCarthy as critic is a delight in pronouncing absolute statements that rest on a kind of brilliant exaggeration. Parts of what she says are usually true, but the truthfulness is sometimes that of a caricature: the salient features are distorted but, through distortion, are emphasized. Like the caricature, the writing calls attention to itself. Doubtless, Miss McCarthy draws with bold, exaggerated strokes so that eyes half-blinded by sentimentalism and uncritical acceptance will see. But at times, overstatement causes the truth, which the reader could accept, to be thrown out along with the bias and exaggeration that he cannot accept.

Although many of the reviews in *Theatre Chronicles* concern unimportant plays that have been forgotten, Miss McCarthy has observed that for her, "in these *ephemeridae*, studied with such care, the America of that time is . . . recaptured: the New Deal years, the war years, the years of Truman" (xv). Interesting as chapters of a social chronicle of this era are reviews of *To Quito and Back* (Ben Hecht), *Pins and Needles* (a Labor Stage production), *The Cradle Will Rock* (Marc Blitzstein), and two Federal Theatre projects—*Prologue to Glory* (E. P. Conkle) and *Haiti* (William Du Bois). Understandably, theater during World War II was poor. Plays of interest reviewed during this period include *Sons and Soldiers* (Irwin Shaw), *Tomorrow the World* (James Gow and Arnauld d'Usseau), *One Touch of Venus* (Ogden Nash, S. J. Perelman, Kurt Weill), *Over Twenty-one* (Ruth Gordon), *Winged Victory* (Moss Hart), and *The Voice of the Turtle* (John Van Druten).

Mary McCarthy comes into her own, however, when she discusses such major figures as Shakespeare, Shaw, Chekhov, Ibsen, and O'Neill. O'Neill provides a suitable test case for he appears in a number of reviews, and Miss McCarthy's treatment of him varies. In the first of these, "Eugene O'Neill—Dry Ice" (November-December, 1946), the playwright is badly abused. O'Neill, Miss McCarthy contends, "is probably the only man in the world who is still laughing at the iceman joke or pondering its implications. He is certainly the only writer who would have the courage or the lack of judgment to build a well-made play around it"

(85). "Well-made" describes *The Iceman Cometh*—not articulate; for in Miss McCarthy's opinion, O'Neill cannot write. Like Farrell and Dreiser, he belongs to a "group of American authors . . . whose choice of vocation was a kind of triumphant catastrophe" and who have succeeded through sheer tenacity (81-82). Thus the problem of judging their work is comparable to that of evaluating "the great, logical symphony of a tone-deaf musician" (82).

Miss McCarthy considers that her "rather bony synopsis" of the plot does *The Iceman Cometh* "perfect justice; in fact, it improves it by substituting, whenever possible, the word *illusion* for the word *pipe-dream*, which recurs with a crankish and verbally impoverished tastelessness about two hundred times during the play" (84). She finds that *The Iceman Cometh* is made maudlin by its linguistic deficiencies: "How is your wife getting along with the iceman, the characters roar, over and over again, and though death is the iceman, the joke is not appreciably refined by this symbolic treatment; rather, it is death that is coarsened" (85).

In a review of *A Moon for the Misbegotten* (New York *Times Book Review*, August 31, 1952, and included in *Theatre Chronicles*, pp. 86-88), Miss McCarthy criticizes the extent to which O'Neill "is taken in by the 'tragic' figure of James Tyrone Jr., who is merely a pitiable wreck" (88). But she considers that the play has a curious mythic power and exacts homage "for the element of transcendence jutting up woodenly in it like a great home-made Trojan horse" (88). "Odd Man In" (Winter, 1959) includes a review of *A Touch of the Poet* that is almost favorable. O'Neill is commended for his honesty and, in the character of Major Cornelius Melody, for the creation of a believable "non-hero."

"The American Realist Playwrights" (July, 1961), an attempt to define realism, discusses Arthur Miller, Tennessee Williams, William Inge, Paddy Chayevsky, and—to provide a historical perspective—Ibsen and O'Neill. In this essay, Miss McCarthy describes O'Neill as a "great figure" looming above the contemporary dramatists; and, although she still does not excuse O'Neill's inarticulateness, she finds in the relentless prose of his last great play, *A Long Day's Journey Into Night*, a peculiar beauty and in the amassing of details an approach to tragedy.

But, she contends, the realist mode generates "a dissatisfaction with itself, even in the greatest masters: Tolstoy, for example, came to feel that his novels, up to *Resurrection,* were inconsequential trifling; the vital truth had been left out" (220-21). For this reason, she explains, after first trying to supply what was missing through symbols, Ibsen attempted to heighten his dramas by forcing the action at the climaxes until finally he renounced "realism in favor of a mixed mode or hodgepodge."

Miss McCarthy then applies this argument to account for the various dramatic experiments of O'Neill who, dissatisfied with verbal poetry as a means of achieving a greater realism, utilized such devices as masks, the aside and the soliloquy, and the framework of myth. Curiously, in *A Long Day's Journey Into Night,* which Miss McCarthy terms "the great play of his old age," O'Neill returned to the straightforward realism of the early plays. If he succeeded "in deepening the character of his realism, it was because the missing element he strove to represent was not, in the end, 'poetry' or 'beauty' or 'philosophy' . . . but simply meaning—the total significance of an action" (224). Meaning or truth, he had come to realize, was embedded in the event itself and could not be abstracted from it.

On other major dramatists, Miss McCarthy is no less interesting in her insights and absolute in her judgments. Shaw's most severe limitation, she explains in "Shaw Off Broadway" (Spring, 1955), is that he considered himself "as a completely rational man—indeed, often, as the only rational man in a world of fools and lunatics" (159). Problems amused Shaw without really engaging his mind and he set them forth as paradoxes or dilemmas, both of which are eternal. "He saw warring antinomies, doomed to everlasting strife, men against women, youth against age, intelligence against stupidity, the few against the many, the artist against the citizen. And the difficulty between them was a failure of communication, that is, of rationality . . ." (159-60). This failure led Shaw to a "nihilistic relativism, in which everyone is right, from his own point of view, and these points of views are isolated, each revolving on its axis in inter-planetary space" (160). Eventually, Shaw became a crank, peddling a series of panaceas that now seem sadly outdated. In her estimation, Shaw, the "most gifted and original playwright of his day" and the "best English playwright since Congreve," failed to achieve greatness "while playing the great man."

"Shaw and Chekhov" (June, 1938) compares not only *Heartbreak House* (1917) and *The Sea Gull* (1896) but the two dramatists as well. The plays share, Miss McCarthy states, only superficial resemblances: the theme of "futility," the dramatization of the decline of a cultured leisure class, a concern with the contradictions apparent in human nature, and the technique of the "confession" to reveal character. The major difference, she finds, is that *Heartbreak House* deals in generalizations whereas *The Sea Gull* concerns particularities. "Shaw's people are thought of as symbols of abstract social ideas; Chekhov's people are observed concretely, and only in the aggregate become symbolic of a social order. Shaw's conception of character is inorganic; Chekhov's organic" (43). Miss McCarthy develops this last idea, pointing out that, while Shaw's "confessions" seem exhibitionistic and artificial, those in Chekhov stem naturally from "an artless preoccupation with the self which runs throughout Russian life and literature." In a review of *The Three Sisters* included in "The Russian Soul in Wartime" (March-April, 1943), she observes that Chekhov's dramatic signature is his "peculiar use of a kind of modified soliloquy to treat the theme of self-consciousness . . ." (60). Although she sees Shaw's failure to equal Chekhov as the result of "a certain coldness and poverty" noticeable in even his best plays, she considers that *Heartbreak House*, because of the eloquence of its style and the nobility of its conception, compares favorably with *The Sea Gull* which, because of the sentimental triviality of its theme, is one of Chekhov's worst plays.

"The Will and Testament of Ibsen" (Winter, 1956) enlarges on the brief analysis of Ibsen found in "The American Realist Playwrights" and seeks to explain the Norwegian dramatist by comparing him with the hero of *The Master Builder* (1892). For example, whereas Master Solness first built churches, Ibsen wrote poetic plays. The construction of houses by the master builder parallels Ibsen's social dramas, as the still later houses with steeples erected by Solness represent the dramatist's late, symbolic plays. In relation to the late nineteenth-century architect-novelists, Miss McCarthy concludes, Ibsen stands only as a "master-builder" whose significant contribution is clinical in nature: "He was the first to put a neurotic woman—Hedda, Ellida Wangel, Mrs. Solness, Nora—on the stage" (178).

Shakespeare is re-interpreted in "General Macbeth" (June, 1962), the last essay in the collection. Macbeth, it seems, is henpecked. He may be "old Iron Pants in the field," but in the castle Lady Macbeth wears the pants. Yet she is more humane and imaginative than her pedestrian husband—"a murderous Babbitt." Macbeth, to Miss McCarthy, is the most modern of Shakespeare's characters—an expert buck-passer, a vicarious creature, a monster only in that he is capable of breeding monsters. *Macbeth* "shows life in the cave. Without religion, animism rules the outer world, and without faith, the human soul is beset by hobgoblins. This at any rate was Shakespeare's opinion, to which modern history, with the return of the irrational in the Fascist nightmare and its new specters of Communism, Socialism, etc., lends support" (247). It is with this irrationality and the false reality of the modern world that the essays in *On the Contrary* deal.

II *As an Essayist*

On the Contrary contains twenty-one essays grouped into three basic categories: "Politics and the Social Scene," "Woman," and "Literature and the Arts." The subtitle, "Articles of Belief, 1946-1961," suggests an underlying unity; all the essays seek to explain events or attitudes characteristic of the post-Hiroshima world. The emphasis is on disclosing the changed shape of reality in a world altered drastically by the atomic and hydrogen bomb and on revealing what, in American culture, seeks to obscure this reality—most notably, in Miss McCarthy's opinion, inertia, cant, sentimentality, and hypocrisy. Arthur Schlesinger, Jr., has noted that "reality, as Mary McCarthy perceives it, "exists in the spontaneities and unpredictabilities of human experience. Yet all of us, she supposes, are engaged for a multitude of reasons in a conspiracy to escape reality, to tame and falsify it. Mankind evidently *can* live by cliché alone. Miss McCarthy's effort is to get us off the stuff and restore the capacity for individual perception."[7] Because reality cannot be separated from an individual's perception of it, Miss McCarthy's vision, which is by definition singular, has "its share of distortions and illusions."[8] *Memories of a Catholic Girlhood* offers help in explaining the singularity of perception evident in *On the Contrary*. Much of Mary Mc-Carthy's need to strip away façades and to uncover what she considers to be the truth is the result of the unusually high value she places on honesty, as the sketches in *Memories* document.

A number of the essays in *On the Contrary* can also be considered autobiographical sketches. "The Vassar Girl" (May, 1951), "My Confession" (Fall, 1953), and "Artists in Uniform" (March, 1953) are clearly chapters in the life history of Mary McCarthy. Like the essays in *Memories of a Catholic Girlhood*, they exhibit self-consciousness, self-scrutiny, and a keen awareness of "surroundings." "Artists in Uniform" is particularly interesting for, as well as revealing the person of the author more fully, it provides subject matter for another essay, "Settling the Colonel's Hash" (February, 1954). The main personages in "Artists in Uniform" are the author, an Air Force colonel, a young man in a Dacron suit, and a mining engineer: all occupants of a club car on a train westbound for St. Louis. Their conversation centers around Communists in the universities, the assumption taken for granted by the three men of the irrevocable entwining of Communism, intellectualism, and Jewishness. The colonel, handsome in his well-tailored uniform, is the ringleader and the most vociferous in airing his anti-Semitism.

When the colonel guesses that Mary McCarthy, toward whom he has taken a proprietary interest, is a sculptress, her casual amusement changes to concern as she sees that the other two men accept this conjecture without hesitation. On that particular day, she recalls, "I was wearing a bright apple-green raw silk blouse and a dark-green rather full raw silk skirt, plus a pair of pink glass earrings; my hair was done up in a bun. . . . Refracted from the three men's eyes was a strange vision of myself as an artist, through and through, stained with my occupation like the dyer's hand. All I lacked, apparently, was a pair of sandals. My sick heart sank to my Ferragamo shoes; I had always particularly preened myself on being an artist in disguise."[9] "Disguised" as a so-called average person, she felt that she was able to speak from the point of view of an artist in such accidental gatherings as this one without her comments appearing to have been prejudiced by her occupation. As an "artist in uniform," she did not possess this freedom.

Unable at last to tolerate the virulent anti-Semitism and stupidity of the three men, she leaves their company to return to her own car where she sits opposite two nuns. Reflecting on the conversation that had just taken place, she wishes that she had made it clear that she "had left the club car for intellectual and principled reasons; I wanted those men to know that it was not I, but my principles, that had been offended." Their probable interpretation of her behavior "voided the whole concept of transcendence, which was very close to my heart, the concept that man is more than his circumstances, more even than himself" (61).

Previously, the colonel had taken for granted that she was to lunch with him in St. Louis, where each had to wait for trains. As a result, she finds herself some time later trying to explain to the colonel why she did not wish to have lunch with him. Finally, exhausted by the heat and the complexity of the situation, she yields to his persuasiveness. During the lunch (she orders a sandwich and he roast beef hash—choices integral to "Settling the Colonel's Hash"), she continues the argument by trying to explain why the Communist movement in America has attracted, relatively, a large number of Jews. Although the colonel is unaffected by what she says, Miss McCarthy sees in the process of arguing that her own defense of the Jews, by affording her superiority to both anti-Semites and Jews, is an exercise in patronage: "There could be no doubt that the Jewish question evoked a curious stealthy lust or concupiscence. I could feel it now vibrating between us over the dark table. If I had been a good person, I should unquestionably have got up and left" (66).

But she stays, although the argument ends only in the colonel's attempt to modify some of his statements after his discovery that his companion is a writer. While she waits on the car's platform for the train to leave, he calls up to her and asks her married name. "Broadwater," she explains. The train starts to pull away from the station. As she looks at the expression on his face, she realizes that to him the name is Jewish, like Goldwater; and she acknowledges that "the victory was his." She watches as he turns curtly away. And so the essay ends.

A number of characteristics that occur frequently in Miss McCarthy's writing are evident in this essay. One is her attempt to be honest, even though, in so doing, she creates an unflattering self-portrait. The woman in the club car and later in the restaurant is not made to appear more virtuous than she is. She is stubborn and cannot countenance stupidity. In addition, she is self-conscious, seeing herself as others see her, aware that the contrasting greens of her skirt and blouse were "growing more and more lurid and taking on an almost menacing light, like leaves just before a storm that lift their bright undersides as the air becomes darker" (57). Also apparent is a penchant for details, as the description of her outfit and of the appearance of the club-car occupants reveals. The dramatic value of this piece comes from the self-exposure that is characteristic of autobiography and from the awareness of "anti-anti-Semitism" as a form of prejudice—the reality uncovered beneath the externals of uniform.

"Letter from Portugal" (February, 1955), "Mister Rodriguez of Lisbon" (August, 1955), "America the Beautiful: The Humanist in the Bathtub" (September, 1947), and "Gandhi" (Winter, 1949) also contain autobiographical elements but to a lesser degree. The first two essays describe contemporary Portugal, "a semi-totalitarian state, with certain positive aspects." "Letter from Portugal," effective in its portrayal of the "actual" Portugal that exists beneath a veneer of progress, illustrates Miss McCarthy's capacity to "see" and to record impressions of a place, an ability evident also in *Venice Observed* and *The Stones of Florence*. "Mr. Rodriguez of Lisbon" is a character sketch of "one of the 'new men' of the Salazar regime" and a description of the housing projects in the Lisbon area. Again Miss McCarthy is quick to discern the reality behind exteriors: the benevolent Mr. Rodriguez is at heart autocratic, and the housing projects too often house the wealthy with political pull and not the Lisbon poor. Such is the "progress" of Portugal.

"America the Beautiful: The Humanist in the Bathtub" is the result of trying to explain America in the year 1947 to the visiting Simone de Beauvoir. The *real* America, Miss McCarthy contends, is not the visible America; for the *real* America is unmaterialistic—not materialistic as so many Europeans too facilely believe. She invites the reader to look into his heart. Such self-searching will disclose, she affirms positively, that the reader neither considers himself to be represented by his possessions nor wishes himself to be so judged. Should the reader agree but argue that although *he* does not care about television sets and cars and refrigerators, *other* people do, Miss McCarthy asks him to answer this question: "But who has ever met, outside of advertisements, a true parishioner of this church of Mammon?" The question is loaded. The colorful language does not permit subtleties. But, *if* Miss McCarthy has succeeded in convincing the reader to conclude that no Americans are materialistic, she then turns the tables by stating: "The only really materialistic people I have ever met have been Europeans" (12). By giving only the outlines of the argument, the black-white fallacy becomes clear. The exaggeration evident in this essay is possibly contrariness for the sake of being contrary. Or it is possibly exaggeration to force the reader (and Simone de Beauvoir) to admit a premise that, in Miss McCarthy's estimation, rights a misconception regarding America and Americans.

"Gandhi" protests the horror of the Indian statesman's murder and the complacency with which persons, like her colleagues at Sarah Lawrence, shrug off such atrocities. Miss McCarthy likens Gandhi's murder to those of Trotsky and Carlo Tresca. The casual acceptance of brutality and man's inhumanity, against which the goodness of a person like Gandhi is no armor, diminishes the horror and significance of the act and blurs the harshness of reality.

A few essays result more from Miss McCarthy's response to a situation than to a physical encounter with persons or places. "A Letter to the Editor of *Politics*" (November, 1946), which concerns the morality of the atom bomb and John Hersey's journalistic rendering of the account, is such an essay. Hersey's "Hiroshima," argues Miss McCarthy, far from being an indictment of atomic warfare, minimizes "the atom bomb by treating it as though it belonged to the familiar order of catastrophes—fires, floods, earthquakes—which we have always had with us . . ." (3). Thus *The New Yorker*, by publishing the Hersey essay in an issue that includes panegyrics to smoked turkey and advertisements of the Hotel Carlyle, smears the outlines of reality by allowing politeness and guilt, triviality and horror to be leveled to size and to become one world.

"No News, *or*, What Killed the Dog" (July, 1952), "The Contagion of Ideas" (Summer, 1952), and "Naming Names: The Arthur Miller Case" (Spring, 1957) concern the Senator Joe McCarthy era and the investigations of the House Un-American

Activities Committee. The first two essays explain the development in American society of an underground man. "No News, *or,* What Killed the Dog," based on a speech given at the American Committee for Cultural Freedom conference in March, 1952, points out that, in general, ideas and works of art are allowed to circulate freely in our society. Unfortunately, this same freedom does not extend to the individual: "Howard Fast may serve a jail term, but his books are in currency. . . . The Communist leaders may be jailed, but the Communist books and pamphlets which constitute, presumably, the theoretic basis for their actions are still available to the public" (34). In Miss McCarthy's estimation, this paradox has caused a drift toward "a society of surfaces" and the growth of underground men who hide beneath an acceptable cover of conformity.

"The Contagion of Ideas," a speech delivered to a group of teachers, also discusses the existence of an underground man—only this time, specifically within schools and universities. The "growth of an underground Communism" has resulted from the ban that prohibits avowed Communists to teach. Such a restriction, Miss McCarthy believes, stems partially from a fear of Communism—a germ phobia that rests on the notion that bad ideas are necessarily more contagious than good and on our own guilty awareness that America is not always the clean-living hero and Russia or other Communist countries the black-hearted villain depicted in pro-West propaganda.

"Naming Names: The Arthur Miller Case" deals with Arthur Miller's attempt to retain his integrity during an investigation of his personal and professional life by the House Un-American Activities Committee. Although Miller had never been a Communist Party member, he talked freely about his past and his interest in the Communist groups; but he drew the line at incriminating others. The reality behind the Arthur Miller case, Miss McCarthy discloses, lies in the recognition that the Committee was not truly seeking information—for there was plenty of testimony against the persons Miller refused to denounce; rather, the Committee was applying a loyalty test in which betrayal was the criterion of good citizenship.

A number of essays in the collection are book reviews. They share, by their directness, the intensity of the essays that concern a situation and reveal, as do the drama reviews, an ability to recognize patterns and to spot falsities. "Mlle. Gulliver en Amérique" (January, 1952) has to do with Simone de Beauvoir's grotesquely distorted impressions of America. Were a Lilliputian to read about his land in *Gulliver's Travels*, Miss McCarthy argues, he would find as great discrepancy as would an American reading Simone de Beauvoir's account. The landmarks and some of the persons and institutions characteristic of America have found their way into Mlle. de Beauvoir's book, but its contents are "all wrong, schematized, rationalized, like a scale model under glass." Mlle. Gulliver has blinded herself willfully to what America really is because, Miss McCarthy reasons, to admit the actual America would be, for a European of egalitarian sympathies, to expose the dilemma of equality and the flaws inherent in the philosophy that he has championed.

"The *Vita Activa*" (October, 1958) is a review of Hannah Arendt's *The Human Condition*, "a long essay on the life of action." In this treatise Miss Arendt divides the *vita activa* (opposed to the *vita contemplativa*) "into three spheres—labor, work, and action, action denoting politics or all the words and deeds of the public realm, where men inter*act* with each other" (156). The arguments by which Miss Arendt builds to her conclusion, that "the life of action" or "the matching of great words with great deeds" is now finished, are outlined briefly in this review.

"Recalled to Life, *or*, Charles Dickens at the Bar" (March, 1953) discusses *Charles Dickens: His Tragedy and Triumph* by Edgar Johnson. This biography is like many on Dickens, Miss McCarthy finds, in that it "reads like the report of some officially constituted commission that hands in its verdict as follows: the deceased is cleared of the charge of sentimentality (finding: healthy emotion), chidden for his domestic conduct, and awarded a place among the world's great authors, in recognition of his social vision" (217). The cautious reaction to Dickens on the part of his biographers results from their astonishment at finding "a *man* entombed in the Westminister Abbey grave" and "a *man* entombed in the novel. . . ."

"An Academy of Risk" (Summer, 1959) is a review of *The Tradition of the New* by Harold Rosenberg, a book of collected essays covering painting, poetry, politics, and intellectual history. The keynote to the collection, Miss McCarthy points out, lies in the word "action," not only in relation to painting—and it was Rosenberg who first applied this term to painting—but to poetry, politics, and drama. This book wins Miss McCarthy's praise, for she finds it objective, that is, honest or in close touch with reality or at least one man's view of reality.

"Tyranny of the Orgasm" (April, 1947) dissects *Modern Woman, the Lost Sex* by Ferdinand Lundberg and Marynia F. Farnham. Miss McCarthy attacks the book by setting down the premises (often false) on which the book rests and the devious route which allows the authors to conclude that the American woman should return to her home and leave the world of business and politics to men. "Up the Ladder from *Charm* to *Vogue*" (July-August, 1950) reviews not books but the women's fashion magazines. In the process of exposing the paradoxical relationship that exists between magazine and audience, Miss McCarthy cheerfully bites the hand that has fed her. From the top of the ladder (*Vogue* and *Harper's Bazaar*) to the middle rungs (*Mademoiselle*) to the bottom of the ladder (*Glamour* and *Charm*) these magazines, in her judgment, offer their readers a false sense of belonging to the chic world and of participating in events of fashion. Exposed too is the cant which fills the pages of these magazines, and the illusionism which is pushed by the lowest, *Charm*, as the only recipe for personal success.

"Settling the Colonel's Hash" (February, 1954), "The Fact in Fiction" (Summer, 1960), and "Characters in Fiction" (March, 1961) deal with the modern novel. These essays, for the reader interested in contemporary fiction and in Miss McCarthy as a novelist, are the most "useful" in the collection. "Settling the Colonel's Hash," given first as a talk at the Breadloaf School of English, in Middlebury, Vermont, uses "Artists in Uniform" as a point of departure. An instructor of freshman English who had assigned this "story" to her class for close critical analysis wrote to Mary McCarthy to ask her to "label" the symbols (the two nuns, the greens and pinks of the author's costume, the colonel, the author's sandwich, and the colonel's hash) since most of the class had decided that the story had symbolic overtones. "'From my standpoint,'" the teacher writes, "'the story was an entirely satisfactory springboard for understanding the various shades of prejudice, for seeing how much of the artist goes into his painting'" (228). Miss McCarthy did not answer the letter, but

"Settling the Colonel's Hash" is a reply to a world that has certainly written to Mary McCarthy: "There were no symbols in this story; there was no deeper level. The nuns were in the story because they were on the train; the contrasting greens were the dress I happened to be wearing; the colonel had hash because he had hash . . ." (229).

"Artists in Uniform" is clearly delineated as a short story, not as an article or essay, by the editors of *Harper's* in whose magazine (February, 1954) this "story" first appeared. As noted earlier, Miss McCarthy herself seems rather lax about the classifying of her magazine pieces and admits that she refers to "Artists in Uniform" as a story because "that was what it was called by *Harper's*. I myself would not know quite what to call it; it was a piece of reporting or a fragment of autobiography . . ." (226). A reader approaching this piece as an autobiographical sketch or an essay would, in all probability, be unconcerned with symbolic meanings. But such a rationalization does not "excuse" the teacher, and certainly it dodges the heart of both essays. For Miss McCarthy's concern in "Settling the Colonel's Hash" is with the exaggerated emphasis placed on finding symbolic meanings, a process which has become, for American readers, "a socially competitive enterprise; the best reader is the one who detects the most symbols in a given stretch of prose" (226). To this process Miss McCarthy calls "halt" and makes some valuable distinctions.

She writes that the whole point of "Artists in Uniform" lies in the fact that what she relates really happened. She wrote it in the first person, mentioned the name she uses as an author, and told the colonel the name of her husband (Broadwater). "When I was thinking about writing the story, I decided not to treat it fictionally; the chief interest, I felt, lay in the fact that it happened, in real life, last summer, to the writer herself, who was a good deal at fault in the incident. I wanted to embarrass myself and, if possible, the reader too" (227). She notes that many of her readers, however, have taken this encounter as fiction, an assumption which puzzles her: "It seemed to them perfectly natural that I would write a fabrication, in which I figured under my own name, and sign it, though in my eyes this would be like perjuring yourself in court or forging checks" (228).

To clarify the misunderstanding between herself and her symbol-hunting audience, she differentiates between natural and literary symbols. The great body of fiction contains "natural symbolism, in which selected events represent or typify a problem, a kind of society or psychology, a philosophical theory, in the same way that they do in real life. . . . This symbolism needs no abstruse interpretation, and abstruse interpretation will only lead the reader away from the reality that the writer is trying to press on his attention" (235). The colonel's hash and the author's sandwich are what each character ordered for lunch and, as such, are natural symbols illustrating the difference in food taste, temperament, and background between Miss McCarthy and the colonel. She chose to select something conventionally feminine while the colonel ordered something conventionally masculine, their selection growing naturally out of circumstances that "made us define ourselves as a woman and a man." The sandwich and hash, then, are special, provisional symbols of the two characters.

In this sense, "all human actions are symbolic because they represent the person who does them" (230). Had the colonel ordered a fruit salad with whipped cream, this choice would have indicated a complexity in his character that his actual selection did not. Likewise, the contrasting shades of green in the author's outfit were, she ruefully discovered, a too representative symbol of her taste in clothes and hence of herself as a person. She had no wish to parade as an artist, but when she chose that particular combination of skirt and blouse and accessories, she had become a symbol of an artist. At the same time, she had picked them because she liked the outfit. The students who wanted the symbols "labeled" were looking for something else. "They were searching for a more recondite significance than that afforded by the trite symbolism of ordinary life, in which a dress is a social badge. They supposed that I was engaging in a literary or artificial symbolism which would lead the reader out of the confines of reality into the vast fairy tale of myth, in which the color green would have an emblematic meaning . . ." (231).

Miss McCarthy goes on to explain that any writing, even reporting, is an act of selection in which "some details are left out as irrelevant (though nothing is really irrelevant)." Those that remain have to stand as symbols for the whole. The art of abridgement is the art of natural symbolism and the basis, therefore, of speech and all representation. While natural symbolism has a centripetal intention and tries to declare what an object is, "literary symbolism is centrifugal and flees from the object, the event, into the incorporeal distance, where concepts are taken for substance and floating ideas and archetypes assume a hieratic authority." In such a "dream-forest, symbols become arbitrary; all counters are interchangeable; anything can stand for anything else" (232).

She discusses, in particular, two examples of what she means by natural symbolism that appear in Henry James's *The Golden Bowl* and in Tolstoy's *Anna Karenina*. The golden bowl in James's novel acts as a symbol of Prince Amerigo and of a marriage that can be considered as an act of acquisition. Both the Prince and the marriage are flawed, a situation represented by the crack in the antique bowl. Miss McCarthy considers the golden bowl appropriate to the theme but maintains that this is a natural symbol which should not be construed as a chalice, a Holy Grail, or a female sex symbol. In the same manner, the train in *Anna Karenina* is necessary to the plot of the novel but is also symbolic, "both of the iron forces of material progress that Tolstoy hated so and that played a part in Anna's moral destruction, and also of those iron laws of necessity and consequence that govern human action when it remains on the sensual level" (236). *Anna Karenina* can be read, however, without the reader's assigning a symbolic value to the train. Every detail in Tolstoy has a "meaningfulness and truth to itself that make it tautological to talk of symbolism . . ." (237). The natural symbolism of James and Tolstoy stands in contrast to the artificial literary symbolism of many contemporary novelists who inject symbols into their work and in so doing obscure reality, leading the reader away from meaning and from life.

Miss McCarthy points out that most of the great authors have had a "philosophy of life" which they wished to communicate to their reading public. And, she insists, it is far less damaging to the integrity of a work of art to disentangle a moral philosophy than to violate the "imagery by symbol-hunting." Ideally, a work of fiction is an organic whole that explains in itself the meaning of the events and images, both of which have sprung from a central theme or parent "idea." Accordingly, Miss McCarthy posits, the reader must look for this parent "idea" which, if he reads "quite carefully and literally what the author says," is usually "in plain view" (237). She then goes back to "Artists in

Uniform" and discusses, in somewhat different terms, the meaning of her encounter with the colonel, noting that only in the act of composition did the details (or natural symbols) involved in this confrontation achieve meaning.

The essay concludes with some general observations about the process of writing. Every story, she explains, is an

> act of discovery. A cluster of details presents itself to my scrutiny, like a mystery that I will understand in the course of writing or sometimes not fully until afterward, when, if I have been honest and listened to these details carefully, I will find that they are connected and that there is a coherent pattern. This pattern is *in* experience itself; you do not impose it from the outside and if you try to, you will find that the story is taking the wrong tack, dribbling away from you into artificiality or inconsequence. (240)

She contends that although outlines and arrangements of symbols may have a certain usefulness "for some kinds of minds" when a writer begins a story, in the end they are inadequate; for the story that does not teach its creator something in the process of the writing is dead before it was begun. "If the story does not contradict the outline, overrun the pattern, break the symbols, like an insurrection against authority, it is surely a still birth. The natural symbolism of reality has more messages to communicate than the dry Morse code of the disengaged mind" (241). A writer must act as both a listener and an observer; and, in this process of paying attention to reality, he must be willing to be surprised at the messages reality sends him. If he is able to get "the messages correctly he will not have to go back and put in the symbols; he will find that the symbols are there, staring at him significantly from the commonplace" (241).

What Miss McCarthy has done in this essay is not only to make a useful distinction between natural and literary symbolism but to give valuable insight into her own fiction. Her observation about O'Neill then applies to herself. The lesson that O'Neill learned is that experience itself contains the meaning. Equally important in understanding the craft of Miss McCarthy's fiction is recognition of the emphasis she puts on paying attention to details and—of course—on being able to see reality clearly.

In general, a critic who is also a writer of imaginative works falls into one of two categories: either he tends to praise what he cannot do as a writer and, as a consequence, to exaggerate the importance of some technical aspects not found in his own writing; or he tends to stress those aspects of craftsmanship which he himself exemplifies and are basic to his fiction. As a critic, Miss McCarthy falls into the second category. Consequently, "The Fact in Fiction" and "Characters in Fiction," excellent as these essays are, tend to support certain aspects of the art of fiction that are the particular strengths of Mary McCarthy as a novelist and short-story writer.

A lot of fuss has been made about the cumbrous burden of facts that her fiction carries. Indeed, one of the criticisms that can be leveled against *The Group* is the cataloguing of details culled from real life—such a heavy reliance that it seems as though life itself had not been strained sufficiently through the refining net of the artist's imagination. But the basic premise of "The Fact in Fiction," a paraphrase of talks given to Polish, Yugoslav, and British audiences in the winter of 1960, is precisely the necessity and value of facts to the novel as an art form. "The distinctive mark of the novel is its concern with the actual world, the world of fact, of the verifiable, of figures, even, and statistics" (250). Different as Jane Austen, Dickens, Balzac, George Eliot, Tolstoy, Dreiser, and Faulkner are "from a formal point of view, they have one thing in common: a deep love of fact, of the empiric element in experience" (251).

Accepting as axiomatic that the characters in a novel must act in accordance with the laws of nature, Miss McCarthy uses the absence of the supernatural to distinguish the novel from the tale, the fable, the romance, and the drama. Consequently, she relegates animals that talk to the fabulist and the *deus ex machina* to the dramatist; for the entrance of a providential figure, from above or below, is a·shortcoming in a novel. For this reason she finds fault with Dickens—one of her favorite authors. Miracles, too, are excluded from the novel. Also, the novel cannot be set in the future "since the future, until it happens, is outside the order of nature; no prophecy or cautionary tale like *1984* is a novel" (252). Even the past, through recession, becomes somewhat unreal, making most historical novels romances —although she finds *War and Peace* an exception. Here Miss Mc-

Carthy breaks her analysis to stress that these distinctions are not pejorative. "I do not mean 'Novel good, fable bad,' merely 'Novel novel; fable fable.' *Candide* is not a novel, but to say so is not a criticism of *Candide*" (253). This analysis, she contends, is only an attempt to explain why the novel is disappearing as an art form.

The next section, which traces briefly the history of the novel, emphasizes the novel's reliance on the facts of the *real* world—even to the claim, as the works of Daniel Defoe illustrate, of being true or factual, and not invented. The "fetishism of fact is generally treated as a sort of disease of realism of which Balzac was the prime clinical exhibit. But this is not the case. You find the splendid sickness in realists and nonrealists alike. *Moby-Dick*, among other things, is a compendium of everything that was to be known about whaling" (258). A similar insistence upon fact is found in *The Brothers Karamazov* when Dostoevsky, before introducing Father Zossima, stops his narrative to discuss the role of the elder in Russian monasteries. Other writers, too, use the excursus, among them Tolstoy in *War and Peace*, Stendhal in *The Charterhouse of Parma*, Mann in *The Magic Mountain*, and Dreiser in *An American Tragedy*.

In many ways, Miss McCarthy continues, the novel resembles the newspaper, not only in the odds and ends of information it contains but in the news items of the day—accounts of crimes, high society, industry, politics, finance, and low life. The books of Dickens record the whole of Victorian society. Similarly, Faulkner in his novels tried to construct the whole of a certain section of Mississippi. For these reasons, she finds that the characteristic tone of even the most serious novels is "one of gossip and tittletattle." Yet the novelist today faces a dilemma, for the essence of scandal is its finiteness. But common sense tells him that, with the threat of total destruction, the affairs of the village or province seem of little consequence. As a result, the writer feels himself parochial and his interest insignificant. In addition, the incredible events of contemporary history have rendered the everyday not merely insignificant but also unbelievable.

Since the universe and the individual exert such contradictory claims, one must be true, Miss McCarthy argues, and the other untrue. Because it is the novelist's job to maintain the truth of the finite, he faces a difficult task: "If he writes about his province, he feels its inverisimilitude; if he tries, on the other hand, to write about people who make lampshades of human skin, like the infamous Ilse Koch, he feels still more the inverisimilitude of what he is asserting. His love of truth revolts. And yet this love of truth, ordinary common truth recognizable to everyone, is the ruling passion of the novel" (267). Therefore, in Miss McCarthy's opinion, "the novel is dying," atrophying because of its inability "to encompass the modern world, whose leading characteristic is irreality," a process against which the frantic injections of myth and symbols are powerless. Despite the gloominess of these observations, Miss McCarthy concludes on an optimistic note, for she cannot, "being human, help feeling that the novel is not finished yet" (270). In this essay, Miss McCarthy is defending her own forte as a novelist. Concerning her comments that the novel stoops to gossip, many of her detractors would agree heartily as they point to themselves or to other acquaintances in Mary McCarthy's *roman à clef* novels and short stories.

If in "The Fact in Fiction" Mary McCarthy sees what she wishes to see, in "Characters in Fiction" she directs her vision with even more purpose. The mid-twentieth century American novel, she observes, contains few memorable characters: the Catholic priests of J. F. Powers, Prewitt in *From Here to Eternity* by James Jones, and Henderson in *Henderson the Rain King* by Saul Bellow. A similar situation exists in England and Europe: "The last great creator of character in the English novel was Joyce. It is the same on the continent. After Proust, a veil is drawn" (274). Paradoxically, the contemporary world, as she points out, is rife with individuals waiting to be committed to immortality by the writer's vision and pen. The very agencies that are the "promoters of conformity in America—bureaucracies public and private and the regimented 'schools' and systems of healing and artistic creation—are themselves, through splits and cellular irritation, propagating an array of social types conforming to no previous standard . . ." (273).

These observations lead Miss McCarthy to conclude that the novel has lost interest in the social. But the social, she notes, has retained an interest in itself as the many books written about society attest: *The Status Seekers* by Vance Packard, *Individualism Reconsidered* by David Riesman, and *The Organization Man* by William H. Whyte to name only a few. Therefore, the causes that will explain the dearth of memorable characters in contemporary fiction must be sought *within* the novel and short story, in the form of a technical or technological crisis. The remainder of the essay is an analysis of this technological crisis.

At this point, Miss McCarthy introduces some comments that illuminate her own fiction. She admits that she would enjoy being able to write like Tolstoy but acknowledges that she cannot: " . . . My typewriter simply balks; it 'sees' differently from me and records what to me, as a person, are distortions and angularities" (275). This inability to "go straight" explains—as does her conviction that "the distinctive mark of the novel is its concern with the actual world"—the emphasis that she places on details. For, if Miss McCarthy is unable to avoid distortion when she attempts to create characters (and in *The Paris Review* interview she states that once she starts writing she cannot help exaggerating), she can at least counteract this impulse by a cataloguing of the external world and gain verisimilitude by establishing a recognizable milieu.

The technical experiments that she finds responsible for having created the impasse "within the art of fiction" have to do with the drift of the novel toward either sensibility or sensation, both of which succeed in annihilating "the sense of character." "In violence, we forget who we are, just as we forget who we are when engaged in sheer perception. Immersed in a picture, an effect of light, or a landscape, we forget ourselves; we are 'taken out of ourselves'; in the same way, we forget ourselves in the dentist's chair" (276). The perceptual screen of a character in a novel of sensation, she adds, is simply more primitive than that of one in a novel of sensibility. "Once these discoveries had been made, however, in the recording of the perceptual field (i.e., of pure subjectivity), the novel could not ignore them; there was no turning back to the objectivity of Tolstoy or the rational demonstrations of Proust" (279).

These same technical discoveries have opened, however, "a curious back door" for novelists interested in character. "That is the entry found by Joyce in *Ulysses*, where by a humorous stratagem character is shown, as it were, inside out, from behind the screen of consciousness. The interior monologue every human being conducts with himself, *sotto voce*, is used to create a dramatic portrait" (280). Thus she terms Joyce "the great ventriloquist of the novel" and praises Molly and Mr. Bloom for being "articulated wholes" and not simply "bundles of vagrant sensory impressions" (280). In contemporary fiction, she notes, the "imitation-from-within" has become "almost standard practice for writers who were impatient with the fragmented impressionist novel and who had assimilated nonetheless some of its techniques" (281).

Concomitant with the "imitation-from-within" technique is the loss of the author's voice. This loss results from a parallel development that can be noted in certain recent works that neither use, outright, the stream-of-consciousness tradition nor display a particularly obvious interest in the mechanics of perception. Yet these novels—such as *Lolita* by Vladimar Nabokov, *Henderson the Rain King* by Saul Bellow, *The Catcher in the Rye* by J. D. Salinger, and *The Group*—are also "impersonations, ventriloquial acts; the author, like some prankster on the telephone, is speaking in an assumed voice—high or deep, hollow or falsetto, but in any case not his own" (282). In such works, style is very important since the book must be written in Holden's or Augie's style; and the author must remain "in character" throughout the narrative "unless he shifts to another style, that is, to another character." The result is the apparent loss of the author's voice, although, as in the stream-of-consciousness novels, the author is only hiding within the consciousness of his character. What has been lost is the author's ability to speak in his own voice or through that of an undisguised alter ego. Whereas "the old authors identified with the hero or the heroine, a sympathetic figure whose dreams and desires resembled the author's own," the modern author not only traverses social barriers but very often invades "the privacy of a soul so foreign or so foetal as to seem beyond grasp" (284). This method lacks straightforwardness. "There is something burglarious about these silent entries into a private and alien consciousness" (282). Or so Miss McCarthy felt when she entered the distorted world of Mulcahy in *The Groves of Academe*.

In the next section of the essay, Mary McCarthy examines what she means by *real* characters and relates the loss of the author's voice to the languishing of the "real people" in a novel. Most often, she contends, the memorable characters are the minor personages of a work of fiction and not the hero or heroine, as the novels of Jane Austen—with such minor characters as Mr. and Mrs. Bennet, Lady Bertram, and Mr. Woodhouse—illustrate. "These beings are much more thoroughly and wonderfully themselves than the heroes and heroines are able to be; the reason for this is, I think, that they are comic" (287-88).

The comic element (and here her argument follows closely that of Bergson in *Laughter*) is that aspect of a human being that is incorrigible and changeless. "What we recognize as reality in these figures is their implacable resistance to change. . . . The capacity to learn, from experience or instruction, is what is forbidden to all comic creations and to what is comic in you and me" (288-89). The comic characters, unlike the hero, are viewed *objectively*, as the reader views members of his family, acquaintances, co-workers—in short, all other human beings.

Opposed to all such personages stands the hero, whom the reader views *subjectively*, as he views himself. Now the hero in a novel develops; that is, he learns. "When we identify ourselves with the hero of a story, we are following him with all our hopes, i.e., with our subjective conviction of human freedom . . ." (289). But the hero, Miss McCarthy argues, is a somewhat idealized figure, someone the reader wishes to be like, an ego-ideal *that he follows with his hopes.* On the other hand, the comic characters resemble those people that the reader sees around him and are real not only in the province of the novel but in the far larger province of the world. The hero lacks this kind of reality. His truthfulness is restricted to the world of the novel and to the reader's fantasies about himself.

Having established, therefore, that the hero represents the reader as he would like to be and the comic characters the people who compose the reader's world, Miss McCarthy then talks about the "old novels" in which "there was a continual fluctuating play between the hero and the 'characters,' that is, between the world as we feel it to be subjectively and the world as we know it as observers" (291). This situation does not exist in the modern novel, for, by and large, there is no hero in the traditional sense. To a large degree, this is the result of the author's having chosen to submerge his voice in that of a character very different from himself—a character who should be treated as an object, not as a subject.

Such "silent entries into a private and alien consciousness" are, Miss McCarthy acknowledges, "laborious; to come at a character circuitously, by a tour de force, means spending great and sometimes disproportionate pains on the method of entry" (282-83). The result is a kind of one-sidedness; the author is left without anyone to speak for him. In the absence of the contrast and suspense that a hero in the traditional sense provides and with only a character—neither hero nor comedian—on whom the author has expended a good deal of energy in trying to treat as a subject (a futile task anyway, in Miss McCarthy's opinion), the comic characters or the real characters have languished. "It would seem . . . that there was a kind of symbiosis between the hero and the 'characters,' that you could not have the one without the others or the others without the one. The loss of the hero upset a balance of nature in the novel . . ." (292).

The essay concludes with the observation that when the contemporary novelist restricts the point of view to that of a character who differs radically from the author, he neglects also the common world that exists between him and his reader, the ordinary habitat of real people who in the novel are the comic characters. This common world is "as queer and empty a place as Dickens' world would be if he had spent eight years recording the impressions of Fagin or the sensory data received by Uriah Heep in the slithery course of a morning's walk" (292). The reality that is obscured by the technique of the contemporary novelist is the reality of the everyday, verifiable world that still exists despite the displacement of traditional values.

III A Meeting Ground

Arthur Schlesinger, Jr., has remarked that On the Contrary possesses "a genuine *moral* quality."[10] And, in "Characters in Fiction," Miss McCarthy's concern with the loss of the author's voice becomes a moral problem. In a world of chaos, if such is the condition of the twentieth-century world, why cannot a novelist bring order? Is not this, after all, the age-old function of art: to arrange meaning from chaos and not simply to render or refract the chaos? The weakening of characterization is the result of a blurring of relationships and a losing sight of reality.

On the Contrary is a singular book, and this is its value; for

Mary McCarthy in this work *does* speak in her own voice. A possible criticism is that some of the essays are marred by the author's self-consciousness—by too many glances in the mirror, as Pamela Hansford Johnson has pointed out.[11] This preoccupation established itself as a characteristic of the author in *Memories of a Catholic Girlhood.* In *The Company She Keeps,* Miss McCarthy's first work of fiction, a similar self-consciousness is evident. But also evident is Mary McCarthy's attempt to describe herself with as much objectivity and with as little mercy as she does the company she keeps.

CHAPTER 4

The Key That Works the Person

SOME OF THE PIECES of *The Company She Keeps* (1942) and *Cast a Cold Eye* (1950) share more of the characteristics of the essay than they do of the novel or short story and appear to be the result less of the author's imaginative faculty than her analytic one. At Vassar College, Mary McCarthy had been told that her mind was essentially critical and that she had no creative talent.[1] Obviously, Miss McCarthy has considerable creative ability, but her critical mind does get in her way as an artist. She acknowledges: "Whatever way I write was really, I suppose, formed critically. That is, I learned to write reviews and criticism and then write novels so that however I wrote, it was formed that way. . . . I *think* that this kind of training really makes one more interested in the subject than in the style."[2]

The emphasis in *The Company She Keeps* and in *Cast a Cold Eye* is chiefly on character. Sometimes the character Mary McCarthy explains is herself, as in "Cruel and Barbarous Treatment," "The Man in the Brooks Brothers Shirt," "Ghostly Father, I Confess" (*The Company She Keeps*), and "The Weeds" (*Cast a Cold Eye*). Other sketches describe persons who exemplify certain character types—"Rogue's Gallery," "The Genial Host," "Portrait of the Intellectual as a Yale Man" (*The Company She Keeps*), "The Friend of the Family," and "The Cicerone" (*Cast a Cold Eye*). This latter group resembles somewhat the seventeenth-century character sketches of such writers as Joseph Hall, Thomas Overbury, and John Earle and are lightly satirical in tone.

Miss McCarthy has explained that when she creates a character (and this is true also when she is describing herself), she tries "to be as exact as possible about the essence of a person, to find the key that works the person both in real life and in the fiction."[3] Such an approach is promising, to be sure, but what actually happens is that the short stories appear at times to be only a compilation of "clues," a series of glimpses of the suspect caught in some revealing action until, finally, enough evidence is accumulated and the character is understood. Also, in the sketches that focus on a person other than herself, the emphasis is less on the character as an individual than on his being a representative type—the Yale man, the gracious host, the friend of the family. Such characterizations put into practice "the chief moral or meaning" of her encounter with the colonel: "you cannot be a universal unless you accept the fact that you are a singular. . . ." ("Settling the Colonel's Hash," [239]). For, in describing the idiosyncratic, she has created also the universal: the singularity that makes Jim Barnett recognizable as an individual is what makes him representative of that class of persons to whom Miss McCarthy has given the general label "the Yale man as intellectual."

"Characters in Fiction" also helps to explain the characters in *The Company She Keeps* and in *Cast a Cold Eye*. For one of the premises basic to Miss McCarthy's argument is that the "real" characters are most often the comic characters who, standing at a distance from the writer, are essentially "objects" as opposed to the hero who is a subject. Miss McCarthy finds that the comic characters of Dickens (such as the Micawbers or Mrs. Gamp) are more "real" than the heroes. But as caricatures or types, such fictional personages—in essence "flat" rather than "round"—bear a startling resemblance to the characters that appear in Mary McCarthy's own novels and short stories. Once again a closed circuit exists between what Miss McCarthy preaches as a critic and what she practices as a writer. In addition, by limiting herself to comic characters who are unaffected by time, she does not have to show development. Explanation *is* sufficient. In fact, to grant her fictional personages the ability to change would move those characters from the classification of "object" to "subject." Thus, given the premise that the incapacity to learn from experience is what is comic in human beings and that "real characterization . . . is seldom accomplished . . . without the fixative of comedy," the characters that Mary McCarthy creates are very "real" indeed.

The "keys" that work the characters in Miss McCarthy's fiction are various. Because she creates persons who are recognizable as representative types, externals provide excellent keys. Again her criticism helps to explain her fiction. As noted in the previous chapter, at the conclusion of "Settling the Colonel's Hash" Miss McCarthy stresses the importance of the writer's being "a listener and observer, who can pay attention to reality, like an obedient pupil, and who is willing, always, to be surprised by the messages reality is sending through to him."

Very obviously, what Miss McCarthy observes and hears is absolutely basic to her fiction. And what can be observed (and, similarly, what can be heard) is the factual, the verifiable. Accordingly, when she emphasizes the importance of "facts" to the novel and short story as art forms, she is describing her own forte as a writer. Facts or externals, in her practice, are a means of characterization. Thus taste becomes particularly useful in explaining a person. Preferences in such visual objects as food and clothing and house or apartment furnishings provide ways to assess a character. For example, the little Cuban cheroots that Alma Fortune favors (*The Groves of Academe*), the Empire sofa in the Sinnotts' living room (*A Charmed Life*), and the recipe for a "quick-and-easy meat loaf" sent to Harald Petersen by his mother (*The Group*) should provide the reader with clues to the fictional person. On a somewhat deeper level, preferences in friends, in diction and in patterns of speech, and in gestures or mannerisms help to explain the character. Thus Ellisons' friendship with Mulcahy (*The Groves of Academe*), Warren Coe's "gee's" and "golly's" (*A Charmed Life*), and Margaret Sargent's poses (*The Company She Keeps*) tell the reader something about each of these fictional beings.

In addition to taste, such matters as heredity, social class, and education help to reveal a person. The somewhat clinical and sterilized result is an accumulation of "keys." But the obvious limitations in this method of characterizing (that is, failure to provide insight into those aspects of a human being for which externals provide no clue—spiritual qualities such as loyalty, generosity, and so on) serve Miss McCarthy's purpose well by insuring what in her estimation is a necessary distance between an author and his "comic" characters.

I *General Concerns of* The Company She Keeps

The Company She Keeps (1942) does for the urban set of the 1930's what *Memoirs of Hecate County* (1946) by Edmund Wilson does for the inhabitants of suburbia. When Cyril Connolly tried to explain Miss McCarthy's *The Oasis* (1949) to English readers, he felt obliged to point out that they "may have to contend with two difficulties": the "alert political-minded rootless urban intelligentsia of New York from which her characters are drawn" and a "certain coldness and inhumanity in the writer which is sometimes a by-product of brilliance."[4] These characteristics of *The Oasis* also mark *The Company She Keeps*. Miss McCarthy has explained that the first chapters in this work were written as short stories: "About half-way through, I began to think of them as a kind of unified story. The same character kept reappearing, and so on. I decided finally to call it a novel, in that it does in a sense tell *a* story, one story. . . . It was when I was doing the one about the Yale man that I decided to put the heroine of the earlier stories in that story too."[5]

In the Foreword of *The Company She Keeps* Mary McCarthy describes these stories as an attempt to define the self—an attempt that fails, ultimately, because the self is not to be found in a book. The emphasis is similar to that of *Memories of a Catholic Girlhood*. The self that is revealed, although as fragmentary as the company she keeps, acts as the central intelligence which helps to define the other characters. During most of the episodes, Margaret Sargent, the autobiographical heroine, is between marriages and adrift in the New York City of the 1930's. Her acquaintances, a strange lot, are as ill at ease among themselves as Margaret Sargent is with them and with herself. But to reject the life that she has chosen and the friends that go with it would be to embrace middle-class existence—a solution she has accepted partially by the time of the last episode, "Ghostly Father, I Confess." The alternative is more deadening than the life to which she is committed. The "company" also shares Margaret Sargent's self-consciousness and censoriousness.

II A Collection of Characters

"Rogue's Gallery," the initial character sketch in *The Company She Keeps,* sets the general pattern for those that follow: first, the physical appearance of the character is described and his function in life classified; next, his relationship to Margaret Sargent is analyzed, and then followed by a delineation of the oddities of his behavior; and, finally, the "key" that explains his particular nature and function is presented. The "action" simply illustrates the behavioral pattern of the specimens Mary McCarthy has categorized ("The Genial Host," "Portrait of the Intellectual as a Yale Man," and so on).

"Rogue's Gallery," written as a personal memoir in the first person, concerns Mr. Sheer, for whom Margaret Sargent is working as a private secretary and cultural standard-bearer. Although a dealer in *objets d'art,* I. F. Sheer, as if to flaunt expectation, is an arrant "con man" who prefers shady deals to legitimate business transactions. Even his preference in art gives him away, for he delights in ingenuity of any kind—"boxes with false bottoms, cuckoo clocks, oval miniatures of the school of Boucher that opened if you pressed a button and disclosed a pornographic scene."[6] Art, to him, was "a splendid confidence game, the craftsman who did not, in some fashion, deceive his public seemed to him a sort of stool pigeon, a high-class rat" (31). Consequently when he achieves outward respectability as a partner in a successful gallery some years later, he resorts to practicing needless deceits. To succeed in one's own personality is odious even to a successful con man. Mr. Sheer, like most of Miss McCarthy's "characters," is a paradox.

Pflaumen, the central character of "The Genial Host," a character sketch told in the second person, is less complex than Mr. Sheer, and Mary McCarthy is able to find the key to his personality more easily. Put very simply, Pflaumen is an emotional and intellectual bore whose particular function in life is that of a host. During the parties that he stages, his well-appointed apartment serves as "a house of assignation, where business deals, friendships, love affairs were arranged, with Pflaumen, the promoter, taking his inevitable cut." The key to Pflaumen's personality is the price that he exacts as host. "The hawklike mouth was not deceptive, for he was a true bird of prey—he did not demand any of the trifles that serve as coin in the ordinary give-and-take of social intercourse; he wanted something bigger, he wanted part of your life" (121). His "inevitable cut" is information concerning the "deal" arranged through his genial auspices. Margaret Sargent knows: "Sooner or later you would break with him. . . . But not yet, not while you were still so poor, so loverless, so lonely. . . . The time after the next, you promised yourself, you would surely refuse" (122). The relationship, commercial and hypocritical, is therefore symbiotic, for Pflaumen is a perfect host.

"Portrait of the Intellectual as a Yale Man," Mary McCarthy has explained, "is not a bit autobiographical, but the heroine appears anyway, in order to make a unity for the book."[7] John Chamberlain, author of *Farewell to Reform* and *The Enterprising Americans,* served as a model for Jim Barnett, the Yale man. Miss McCarthy attempted in this episode "to make this real man a broad type. You know, to use John Chamberlain's boyish looks and a few of the features of his career, and then draw all sorts of other Yale men into it."[8] Chamberlain, however, has denied the generalization implicit in the title: "Thomas Beer, Sinclair Lewis, Waldo Frank, George Soule, Selden Rodman, Archibald Mac-Leish, Dean Acheson, Max Lerner, John Hersey and Dwight Macdonald are all identifiable as Yale 'intellectuals'—but just what common denominator makes them a 'broad type'?"[9]

Margaret Sargent was put into this story, Miss McCarthy adds, "in an imaginary love affair, which *had* to be because she had to be in the story. I always thought that was all very hard on John Chamberlain, who was married. But of course he knew it wasn't true, and he knew that I didn't know him very well, and that therefore in the story he was just a kind of good-looking clothes-hanger."[10] This reasoning on the part of Miss McCarthy is peculiar, to say the least, in view of the concern she shows in *Memories of a Catholic Girlhood* and in the autobiographical sketches of *The Company She Keeps* for her image in the eyes of others. But John Chamberlain, some twenty years later, does not seem particularly concerned about his portrait: "Since my own identification with the Left in those days was purely out of a depression-induced pessimism . . . , I have never been able to see myself in Jim Barnett's shoes. I thought socialism was a stomach appeal, and said so. Where Jim Barnett 'sold out,' I merely recovered my optimism—or maybe it was my nerve."[11]

The portrait of Jim Barnett as intellectual is distinctly un-flattering: he is the Average Thinking Man turned Marxist. Not only that, he has a small soul. A middle-of-the-road liberal, he commits himself to no faction. His wife, by looking "too much like her mother, which was a very bad thing in a girl," illustrates his basically reactionary nature. It is the old story of the leopard being unable to change his spots. Jim Barnett never renounced his birthright by becoming a liberal, and the spots began to re-appear when the pose became tiresome. John Chamberlain has analyzed a "lack of fundamental seriousness" as the flaw in the character of Jim Barnett that Mary McCarthy found most detest-able.[12] And this failure is the key that works this particular character type.

The common denominator, for Miss McCarthy, that makes the Yale man a category is a reluctance to embrace any doctrine wholeheartedly—a fear of systems. In "Portrait," the Trotsky issue (on which Jim Barnett sided with Margaret Sargent and which resulted in his leaving the *Liberal*) is a red herring—an excuse for Jim's getting back into the cozy arms of capitalism and not a cause that he championed out of a heart-felt conviction. Once entrenched in the suburbs and secure as a staff writer on a business magazine, he seldom sees Margaret and the company she keeps, "the unsuccessful, opinionated, unknown intellectuals."

Still, when Jim and Margaret meet at parties, her presence makes him feel the failure of his own life and the limitations of his own nature: "That single night and day when he had been almost in love with her had taught him everything. He had learned that he must keep down his spiritual expenses—or else go under" (181). The love affair between Margaret and Jim, otherwise insipid and of little interest, is significant in that it allows the reader to see Margaret Sargent as Jim Barnett sees her or as Miss McCarthy *thinks* Margaret appears to the Yale Man as Intellectual. The characterization that results dramatizes the curious mixture of bravado and uncertainty, intensity and pas-sivity, tension and abandonment that gives Margaret Sargent complexity.

Cast a Cold Eye (1950) has a wider scope than *The Company She Keeps* as the two character sketches in this later collection illustrate. The first of these, "The Friend of the Family," concerns suburbia, "the long war of marriage," and "the battle of the friends."[13] The beginning sentences establish the dreary tone and allegorical quality of this portrait: "His great qualification was that nobody liked him very much. . . . Consequently, among the married couples he knew, he was universally popular. Since nobody cherished him, swore by him, quoted his jokes or his political prophecies, nobody else felt obliged to diminish him. . . ." The key to the person of Francis Cleary is this very innocuousness. He offends neither husband nor wife because he is a matter of indifference to them. A symbol of compromise, he becomes the "friend" of the family.

Although circumscribed, the world of the hypothetical husband and wife in this sketch is infinitely social. And like any such world, it has its own institutions and its own laws. Characteristic of the setting of "The Friend of the Family" is that concealment and compromise lie at the basis of its primary institution, marriage. Consequently, it is both fitting and necessary that friends of the family—as represented by the single Francis Cleary or by the Francis Clearys as a married couple—are chosen not out of love or admiration but for their neutrality. Part of the key to the friend of the family lies in recognizing that he is an inevitable by-product of the world that Mary McCarthy describes in this sketch.

Although "The Friend of the Family" begins in the third person, Miss McCarthy quickly moves to the more familiar "we" and "our" as she invites the reader to share her opinions about the husband and wife and about Francis Cleary. Then, discarding the first person plural, she adopts the even more familiar "you," thereby drawing the reader into the episode by forcing him to see himself in Francis Cleary and in the husband and wife whose marriage she has described. At the conclusion, she has the husband (and, through identification, the reader) ask himself why he and his wife should not become the next Francis Clearys of their social set: "Why should you shrink from it? What have you to lose? In what do you differ from the man on the sofa?" (56). Thus, the key that unlocks "the friend of the family" opens also the closed door of the family circle.

Milan, Venice, Florence, and Rome provide the setting for "The Cicerone." The cicerone of this piece is Rino Sciarappa, an Italian of indeterminate age, whom the two Americans (a young woman and man traveling together) promptly nickname "Scampi" in reference to his favorite dish—fried crayfish-tails. The Americans, who remain unnamed throughout this sketch, find their guide as puzzling as Europe itself, and they are as curious to discover the key to his mysterious ways as they are desirous to understand the Continent. For, in Scampi, they believe, lies "the mystery of Europe." Their various attempts to trap the Italian into revealing himself are, however, unsuccessful. In Rome (Scampi had left them by this time), believing both naïvely and accurately that architecture "explains" a person and a nation, they seek out the Italian's house. But they are disappointed, for his habitation fails to offer a key to the inner man. Such an external can turn the lock only half-way. Although their search gives them an incomplete understanding of their guide and hence of Europe, their experiences provide them with a key to their own behavior which they have begun to realize is as gauche and inadequate as that of a fellow American of their acquaintance—Polly Grabbe.

III *A Strange Interlude*

Written through the central intelligence of a young man, "The Old Men," also in *Cast a Cold Eye*, can be classified neither as a character sketch nor as autobiography despite the protagonist's sharing with Mary McCarthy her curiosity about people and her feminine passivity. The young man (unnamed) is in a New England country hospital where, for several days, he has been waiting to have a fractured elbow set. In the dirty, poorly run hospital, he feels without identity and substance. Accordingly, he becomes involved mentally in the lives of the other patients, particularly the noisy and unruly old men across the hall from him; and he begins to construct a philosophy from what he imagines to be their situation.

From the old men's play-acting (for such, he assures himself, is the cause of the various noises that he hears), he conjectures that man is not sustained by a belief in the self but by a recognition that life rests on artifice. To exist, therefore, involves "an act of deliberate impersonation" which, paradoxically, is capable of creating real life. The cries of a woman patient who, he believes, is suffering from cancer give him additional insight into "some darker reality" that "had been threatening him, he now perceived, from childhood" (88). He equates the screams of the woman with the actual and reasons that " 'the actual, in fact, is *that which should not be witnessed*' " (92).

Buoyed by his new understanding, he determines to live "selfishly and inconsiderately, like the expressive old men; the actual no longer drew him with its womanish terrors and mysteries, its sphinx-rebuff and *invidia* [ill-will]" (92). He sings the epitaph engraved on William Butler Yeats's tombstone: "Cast a cold eye on life, on death, . . . Horseman, pass by.' "[14] In high spirits, the young man promises himself that he will leave the hospital without having the operation and return to Cambridge. But his elation is short-lived when he discovers that his conjectures about the identity of the woman patient are erroneous—as are the conclusions that he had drawn.

Defeated, he agrees to have his arm set later that same day. A few minutes before the operation, he becomes further disillusioned by finding out that the ringleader of the old men had been discharged. This absence negated the possibility of checking his theories concerning artifice and impersonation against the solidness of reality. "Fifteen minutes later, the young man expired under the anesthetic, before the operation proper had begun, the first case of its kind, as Dr. Z explained to Mrs. X, that he had ever come across in his entire practice, where the heart, without organic defect, sound as a bell, in fact, simply stopped beating" (96). On this note, the story ends.

"The Old Men" is clearly not a character sketch, for the emphasis is less on the young man than on his conjectures about the nature of existence—theories, Miss McCarthy implies, that are meaningless flights of fancy because they are not grounded in "reality." As in most of Miss McCarthy's short fiction, a revelation has taken place; but this time, not an unveiling that has to do with the mysteries of a single specimen of humanity but with the mysteries of existence itself and the insufficiency of theoretical knowledge to sustain man in any meaningful way.

IV   *The Autobiographical Heroine and*
The Company She Keeps

In the episodes in *The Company She Keeps* that have to do almost entirely with Margaret Sargent, the search for the self comes more clearly into focus. Mary McCarthy has described "Cruel and Barbarous Treatment," the first of these sketches, as a "stylization—there were no proper names in it or anything—but still, it was an attempt to be as exact as possible about something that had happened."[15] In this episode, the heroine, referred to as She (throughout this account Miss McCarthy uses capital letters, a stylistic device retained partially in this retelling and analysis), is on the verge of divorce: "She could not bear to hurt her husband. She impressed this on the Young Man, on her confidantes, and finally on her husband himself. The thought of Telling Him actually made her heart turn over in a sudden and sickening way, she said" (9). The trite phrases, which are also capitalized, are the language of the heroine and her acquaintances and become a secular refrain. Like the ecclesiastical and the classical allusions, they provide a frame of reference. But instead of deepening the character, they limit the young woman by revealing what is superficial in her nature and in her milieu.

Mary McCarthy is describing a new kind of courtship, one that has become increasingly a pattern of contemporary living. For divorce is usually no longer a scandal, but a way of life. As documented in "Cruel and Barbarous Treatment," the courtship assumes three distinct phases: the Pre-Announcement, the Announcement, and the Post-Announcement. The Pre-Announcement Period is the most exciting of the three for the heroine and the Young Man, for secrecy lends enchantment and affords superiority. Since only she and the Young Man know of their affair, public appearances entail certain calculated risks and test each participant's ability to dissemble. After one particularly effective performance, the heroine gloats over her virtuosity, telling the Young Man that she should have been an actress or an international spy or a diplomat's wife. This curious foreshadowing (for Miss McCarthy later married James West, a State Department official) occurs also in "Ghostly Father, I Confess."

Soon, however, the excitement of the Pre-Announcement period begins to wear thin, and the lovers agree "that The Situation Was Impossible, and Things Couldn't Go On This Way Any Longer." The heroine realizes that to be a "Woman With A Secret" is not satisfying enough, if to acquaintances she appears to be a woman without a secret. Promptly, close friends are informed and their reactions judged. "It was a pity, she reflected, that she was so sensitive to public opinion," knowing that she could not love a man unless everyone else thought him wonderful too (13).

Finally, the time arrives for her to make the Announcement. The confidences to friends appear "like pale dress rehearsals of the supreme confidence she was about to make," and she becomes unbearably curious about "How Her Husband Would Take It." Only when love is faced with its own annihilation, she reasons, can it reveal itself completely. Accordingly, she considers that the Announcement is a test of her husband's love. Judging that her husband would be able to control his feelings better in public, she chooses to make the Announcement at breakfast and selects a fashionable restaurant as the setting. The staging is effective. After the Announcement, he calls for the check immediately; and, hand in hand, they hurriedly leave the restaurant. With tears streaming down their faces, they walk to a public park where, in a nicely ironic mock-pastoral setting, they watch ducks swimming about in an artificial lake. When, at last, her husband responds to her protests of love by saying that he understands, she feels that, through his forgiveness and surrender, she has drawn him into a "mystical union" and that their "marriage was complete."

By comparison, the Post-Announcement Period proves flat. From the onset, her husband behaves calmly, and she senses in his detachment an irony indicating that the Announcement has, in some way, revealed her to him. Her final leave-taking is strained and uninspired. But caught in a world of her own making, she has to abide by its unwritten code and, however unwillingly, go through with the divorce and make the trip to Reno. En route westward, knowing that she would never marry the Young Man for she had grown to detest him, she contemplates her future as a single woman and wonders how she could have forgotten the terror of spinsterhood. She knows that she will always stay a little too late at cocktail parties, hoping to be invited for dinner afterwards. If no invitation is given, she will have to face the prospect of walking out alone while trying to give the impression that she has another engagement. Her imagination stirs up images of dinners in tearooms with women who are also single because women alone look less conspicuous in tearooms than they do in good restaurants.

Finally optimism replaces depression and she envisions herself a *femme fatale,* a woman of the world for whom provisions against old age and loneliness appear Philistine and irrelevant. Enlivened by this new self-image, she examines the other passengers on the train and contemplates what reply she would give if questioned as to her destination. Reno, she decides, would be too direct and leave her cheapened and vulnerable, and San Francisco would not only be dishonest but would make her seem "an ordinary traveler with a commonplace destination." She searches for a middle ground that "would hint at a *vie galante*" while indicating "a barrier of impeccable reserve." Deciding to say simply "West," she reasons that if questioned more specifically, "she might go as far as to say 'Nevada.' But no farther" (22).

Apparent in this sketch is the self-consciousness noticeable in *Memories of a Catholic Girlhood* and in certain of the essays in *On the Contrary.* But the self-awareness of Margaret Sargent results less from the fear of appearing ridiculous than from an anxiety about the role she has chosen to play. Like all persons unsure of their place, she understands who she is—or more importantly *what* she is—by gauging the reactions of other people. Many times, she literally sees herself as others see her. Also, since the role that Margaret Sargent plays has virtually no predecessors, society exhibits a similar self-consciousness. For the middle class has traditionally denied women the freedom of movement that Margaret has won at the price of defiance, an attitude still evident in many of her subsequent actions. In addition, not only does she attempt to live without the more or less stabilizing influence of a husband, but she carries over a vestige of conscience from her middle-class inheritance and a few impractical notions of the "perfectibility" of man from her humanistic education—and these complicate her life still further.

Accordingly, certain situations worry her because she considers "good manners" important. Knowing how to comport herself at a cocktail party is as necessary to Margaret Sargent as the etiquette of introductions to the hostess of a formal reception. So is the knowledge of how to act when a stranger on a train asks her to have a drink with him. But no book of etiquette is available to instruct her. Consequently, she fights between reason and impulse; she is aware as she is struggling inwardly that impulse will win out and knows, too, that a moral issue lies at the root of how she should act.

Like "Cruel and Barbarous Treatment," "The Man in the Brooks Brothers Shirt" details a new kind of courtship. Concerning the "factuality" of the latter episode, Miss McCarthy has explained that she attempted "to describe something that really happened—though naturally you have to do a bit of name-changing and city-changing."[16] In this story, perhaps the most successful in the collection, something *does* happen. Margaret Sargent allows herself to get picked up by the man in the Brooks Brothers Shirt.

Indicative of the rootless world in which the heroine moves is the train that is taking her to Portland, Oregon, ostensibly for the purpose of telling an aunt of plans to be married again. When a new man enters the car, Margaret Sargent appraises him hopefully but finds that he, like the other passengers, is Out of the Question: "He looked, she decided, like a middle-aged baby, like a young pig, like something in a seed catalogue" (63).

But the courtship proceeds anyway along lines determined by the situation: the initial "sizing up" is quickly followed by the approach which, in turn, leads to the proposal—in this instance, a pre-lunch drink in the man's compartment. The acceptance follows next: "A compartment was something she had not counted on. But she did not know (she never had known) how to refuse" (67). In her inability to refuse, Margaret is very much like the heroines of Mary McCarthy's novels, such as Martha Sinnott who cannot reject Miles Murphy (*A Charmed Life*) or the various heroines of *The Group* who are gluttons for new ideas or new gadgets and, in some instances, "new" men. Margaret Sargent's unwillingness to turn down an invitation is simply another indication of her insecurity and unfulfillment.

In the man's compartment, with the door left open, Margaret finds herself enjoying the highballs which "tasted, as her own never did, the way they looked in the White Rock advertisements." The man's efficiency in deploying his brown calf luggage pleases her, as does his attitude toward the waiter; and she discerns in the glances of other passengers "envy, admiration, and censure. . . . The man sat at ease, unconscious of these attentions, but she kept her back straight, her shoulders high with decorum, and let her bare arms rise and fall now and then in short parabolas of gesture" (68).

Part of the search for the self involves finding someone who will be able to explain that self; and, for a while, the man in the Brooks Brothers shirt seems to Margaret Sargent such a person. As the long whiskey-drinking afternoon takes on more and more the qualities of a secular confession, they talk intimately about their marriages. When the man points out that he thinks that she still loves her former husband, she questions him eagerly, believing that she has found the person "who could tell her what she was really like. . . . If she once knew, she had no doubts that she could behave perfectly; it was merely a question of finding out. How, she thought, can you act upon your feelings if you don't know what they are? As a little girl whispering to a young priest in the confessional she had sometimes felt sure." By rejecting the Church and "her aunt's illiterate morality, she had given away her sense of herself" (78).

But the man's reply falls short of comprehending the complexities of her marriage. Later, during dinner in the compartment, she finds herself explaining in erotic detail the intricacies of her former marriage. And then she hears herself asking if he knows her favorite quotation and realizes that she is getting drunk: "*I must not quote poetry,* she thought, *I must stop it; God help us, if I'm not careful, we'll be singing Yale songs next.*" But she cannot stop herself and is capable only of hearing her voice as though she and it were separate. " 'It's from Chaucer,' she went on, when she saw that she had his attention, 'Criseyde says it, *I am myn owene woman, wel at ese.*'" The man, when he finally makes sense of the Middle English, looks at her admiringly. " 'Golly,' he said, 'you are, at that!'" (80-81).

After this speech, the time shifts abruptly to the following morning. Margaret awakens drowsily convinced that Nothing Had Happened and that she is in her own lower berth. Still half-asleep, she moves and touches the naked body of the man. Events of the previous night come back to her memory hazily: the closed door, their singing, and then the man trying to kiss her. "She had fought him off for a long time, but at length her will had softened," and they had made love, somewhat peculiarly, she now thinks. The comfort of vagueness lasts for only a short while as exact and painful details flood into her consciousness. "There were (oh, holy Virgin!) four-letter words that she had been forced to repeat, and, at the climax, a rain of blows on her buttocks that must surely (dear God!) have left bruises" (82).

Hurriedly she tries to dress, hoping to get back to the Pullman before either the man or the other passengers waken; but the man's sudden awakening and his demand that she kiss him destroy the possibility of an easy escape. Sudden nausea overcomes her, and she pulls away from his embrace: "He pointed to the toilet seat, which was covered with green upholstery. . . . She raised the cover and vomited, while the man sat on the bed and watched. This was the nadir, she thought bitterly; surely nothing worse than this could ever happen to her. She wiped the tears from her eyes and leaned against the wall" (84). Afterwards, troubled by a feeling that she was "as hard as nails," she agrees to make love. "*This*, she thought decidedly, *is going to be the only act of charity I have ever performed in my life; it will be the only time I have ever given anything when it honestly hurt me to do so*" (87-88). As she waits impatiently "for the man to exhaust himself," she imagines herself a sacrificial lamb and finds pleasure at her selflessness and goodness.

In New York City, she and the man continue their affair (she had decided again not to get married), but their differences make its rapid dissolution inevitable. From the start, he had been Out of the Question (his emblemed shirt had accurately given him away). When her father dies some time later, the man sends a telegram which reads: "SINCEREST CONDOLENCES. YOU HAVE LOST THE BEST FRIEND YOU WILL EVER HAVE." Instead of filing this telegram with the other messages, she tears it up carefully and throws it into the wastebasket, reasoning that "it would have been dreadful if anyone had seen it" (102). To the end, although still unsure of herself, as indicated by her relentless self-consciousness, she remains nonetheless an opponent of the bourgeois sentimentality represented by the message of the telegram.

Also apparent in this account is another element found in the writing of Mary McCarthy: the sexual passivity of her heroine.

Miss McCarthy's typical female character usually finds herself being pushed rather unwillingly into bed. And, even during sexual intercourse, the heroine does not stop *thinking*, or so it seems. For example, while Margaret Sargent is envisioning herself as a sacrificial lamb, she also sees herself dressed once again and back safely in her own Pullman seat, reading the novel she had brought with her. Additionally, although Miss McCarthy's heroines are not aggressive sexually, they are provocative in actions and words. The cerebral intent of their flirtatious behavior is, however, curious.

Elizabeth Hardwick finds the frankness of Mary McCarthy's description of sexual encounters in direct contrast with "the hot prose of male writers. . . . In her fiction, shame and curiosity are nearly always found together and in the same strange union we find self-condemnation and the determined pursuit of experience; introspective irony and flat, daring action."[17] Part of the original contribution of Mary McCarthy, Miss Hardwick claims, is "to have written, from the woman's point of view, the comedy of Sex. The coarse actions are described with an elaborate *verismo* of detail."[18] What helps to make these scenes comic, apart from the heroine's stubborn pursuit of adventure, is her persistence in retaining an image of herself and her bedfellows, so that their various weaknesses are displayed publicly against the setting of an act that society has deemed private. The effect is ludicrous. Also there is an almost comic innocence in Margaret Sargent's feeling that her sexual encounter with the man in the Brooks Brothers shirt is the nadir of her life and that she could experience no greater horror. "The worst is not so long as we can say 'This is the worst,'" says Edgar in *King Lear*. Margaret Sargent's "fall" is, in actuality, only the moral pratfall of high comedy and not an experience in Evil as her overactive imagination first envisions it to be.

In "Ghostly Father, I Confess" the attempt to find the key that works the self is more deliberate. The title comes from a fifteenth-century anonymous religious lyric prefaced to the story. The allusion to the Father-Confessor of the Roman Catholic Church is ironic. In the secular world Margaret Sargent inhabits, the priest-confessor has been replaced by the psychoanalyst. And it is to him that Margaret Sargent must now confess the kiss of doubtful rather than "grete" sweetness that she has stolen so ill-advisedly and that is "doon not undoon now."

To the reader of *Memories of a Catholic Girlhood,* much of the information in "Ghostly Father, I Confess" that has to do with the childhood of Margaret Sargent is repetitious. Only some changes in names and setting have occurred. Once the proper "real" life identifications have been made, the lines of auto-biography emerge clearly. In this episode, Margaret Sargent is financially secure, for she is married unhappily to a successful but domineering architect. "If she could have been very rich— It was the ugly cartoon of middle-class life that she detested, Mr. and Mrs., Jiggs and Maggie, the Norths in the *New Yorker.* And the more stylish you tried to make it, smearing it over with culture and good taste, Swedish modern and Paul Klee, the more repellent it became . . ." (190). Also, she no longer believes herself indestructible: "The little apartment in the Village, the cocktail parties, the search for a job, the loneliness, the harum-scarum, Bohemian habits, all this was now unthinkable for her. She had lost the life-giving illusion, the sense of the clean slate, the I-will-start-all-over-and-this-time-it-is-going-to-be-different" (203-4).

The only solution is to discover a way of dealing with the present situation. Her sessions with the analyst indicate a means of salvation, a "key" that will explain her behavior. Her marriage to Frederick, Dr. James counsels, is a re-enactment of certain childhood relationships, and he advises her to win her freedom from Frederick as she had won her freedom from her father and her aunt. After the session ends, she walks down Madison Avenue, remembering a dream that she had started to tell the analyst. In this dream, she was at an outing cabin with two other girls (who were also students at Eggshell College) and "three tall young men, all of them a sort of dun color, awkward, heavy-featured, without charm, a little like the pictures of Nazi prisoners . . ." (221).

When one of the young men approached her, she became animated and flirtatious despite her resolve to take no part in the evening's "fun" and told one of the girls: " 'Really he is not so bad as the others. He is quite interesting when you begin to talk to him.' " But, when he kissed her coarsely and brutishly, she looked up and saw that his handsomeness had disappeared. Then, as she watched, he once again metamorphosed into a

Byron-like figure: "When he kissed her this time, she kept
her eyes shut, knowing very well what she would see if she
opened them, knowing that it was now too late, for now she
wanted him, anyway" (222).

The dream, she realizes, is significant—"it was some failure in
self-love that obliged her to snatch blindly at the love of others,
hoping to love herself through them, borrowing their feelings,
as the moon borrowed light. She herself was a dead planet."
And she sees that the Nazi prisoner and the Byronic impostor
are parts of her own equivocal nature. But at least, she consoles
herself, she is still able to detect her own frauds; she had been
able to know, even with her eyes closed, when the young Nazi
had ceased to be Lord Byron. She prays to be allowed to retain
the ability to see with an inner spiritual eye and asks to be preserved in this disunity between flesh and spirit. " '*O di*,' she said
aloud, '*reddite me hoc pro pietate mea!* [O ye Gods, grant me
this in return for my piety].' " The favor she asks is small, "but,
like Catullus, she could not be too demanding, for, unfortunately,
she did not believe in God" (222-23).

V   *Foreign Phrases and the Matter of Style*

The use of ecclesiastical allusions and foreign phrases, particularly Latin, is a characteristic of Mary McCarthy's prose style.
She admits that "at their worst they're rather just literary references. That is, slightly show-off literary references. I have a
terrible compulsion to make them—really a dreadful compulsion.
. . . I think I do it as a sort of secret signal, a sort of looking over
the heads of the readers who don't recognize them to the readers
who do understand them."[19] Her use of Latin—which, as she has
said, came fluently to her—reflects easy familiarity and suggests
that she works from memory. Sometimes her quotation differs
from that of the original; the last line, for example, of Catullus's
poem 76 reads: "*reddite mi hoc*" not "*me*" as it appears in Miss
McCarthy's version. Most often the Latinism that she uses has no
exact English equivalent; *invidia*, for example, can be translated
as "ill-will" but this does not encompass the range of appropriate
synonyms—envy, grudge, spite, spitefulness, jealousy, odium, and
unpopularity are all possible equivalents. Connotatively, *invidia*
carries with it the collective force of all these synonyms. Also,

since she writes about "educated" people and to an "educated" audience, the Latin phrases have an appropriateness. She draws from both classical and secular sources (Catullus, Horace, Cicero, Caesar, and Terence) and ecclesiastical (mainly from the litany of the Roman Catholic Church). Her translations, when she does include a translation in the text, are free and indicate a "feeling" for the language.

Mary McCarthy has said that she has "never liked the conventional conception of 'style.' What's confusing is that style usually means some form of fancy writing. . . . But if one means by style the voice, the irreducible and always recognizable and alive thing, then of course style is really everything. It's what you find in Stendhal, it's what you find in Pasternak."[20] It is in this larger sense that "style" is being used in this critique. Her prose contains a mixture of polysyllabic abstract words of Latin origin and of shorter, concrete Anglo-Saxon ones. This "mixed diction" allows both preciseness and flexibility. Another curiosity about Mary McCarthy as a writer is that she emerged into print as an excellent stylist and has remained one. The improvement in her later writing lies only in a deepening and enlarging of wit and in a lessening of rhetorical flourish.

VI *The Autobiographical Heroine and "The Weeds"*

"The Weeds" (*Cast a Cold Eye*) carries over the heroine of *The Company She Keeps*. The wife in "The Weeds" (although she is never named) is married unhappily to an architect, paralleling the situation of Margaret Sargent in "Ghostly Father, I Confess." In contrast to Margaret, however, who had only talked about leaving Frederick, the wife in "The Weeds" does leave her husband and the flower garden that she had cultivated so avidly. But she finds New York City a disappointment. The five years that she had lived in the country had made her a visitor. Her friends, she discovers, "had forgotten her, forgotten, that is, her former self, which remained green only in her own memory; for her alone, time had stood still" (16). Caught by inertia, she hunts for a job haphazardly, and spends a large part of each day in her hotel room, reading the Gideon Bible.

In "Ghostly Father," Margaret had discovered that, although she was not free, her husband, by assuming the role of dictator, had assumed also absolute guilt. As a consequence, she felt herself absolved from her own wrongdoings. The heroine of "The Weeds," alone in her hotel room, realizes somewhat belatedly that her flight had caused her to exchange "the prison of the oppressor for the prison of the self, and from this prison there was not even the hope of escape" (19). Bereft of a scapegoat, she recognizes her own inadequacies with an overly severe and debilitating clarity.

On the fourth day of her escape, her husband telephones, but she refuses to meet him. By the sixth day, she assumes that he has left the city, and her spirits brighten. She decides to take action by talking with a friend in advertising. As she rides down in the hotel elevator, she imagines what answer she would give when asked why she had left her husband. A sentence comes to mind that delights her: "She foresaw a whole train, a lifetime, of these sentences. . . . She smiled, feeling herself on home territory. She was back at her port of embarkation, which she had set forth from five years before, back to her native patois, where jest masks truth but does not deny it" (20). And then, when she steps off the elevator, she sees her husband.

Sullenly, she returns to the house in the country; but she refuses to inspect the garden and takes no interest in the details of running the household. At last, yielding to her husband's repeated requests, she does go out to the garden, but, as she has feared, the weeds had triumphed: "solidly before her lay the brutal *fait accompli,* the lost garden, irrecoverable, . . . the mirror of absolute beauty in which she had glimpsed her own image, was shattered" (24). Aware that "the part of her which regarded nothing as final, which was continually planning, contriving, hoping" had been lost, she finds herself, a few weeks later, accepting her husband's avowal that he has always liked her flowers. She recognizes that he is lying, but she knows also, with a sudden clarity, that he cannot be made to believe differently: ". . . In a final thrust of rejection, she yielded, conceding him everything—flowers, facts, truth. Let him put them into his authorized version; she had failed them, and would do so again and again" (31). Agreeing with his lie, she finds, is easier than she had thought possible.

Margaret Sargent, in "Ghostly Father, I Confess," had also been aware of a gradual dulling of her sensibilities. Psychoanalysis had succeeded in making her cognizant of the possibilities of hypocrisy: "And why mention to your husband that you have spent too much money on an evening dress, gone to the races and lost, had too much to drink, let a man kiss you in the pantry? Pay your debt with the housekeeping money, take your mother's bracelet to the pawnshop, stifle the hang-over with Benzedrine, say the ice tray stuck and you were a long time getting it out. Do, in other words, what every normal wife does, agree and go your own way. . . ." The heroine in "The Weeds" puts this lesson into practice.

"The Weeds" is a bleak story precisely because in it honesty and hypocrisy triumph over sincerity and truth in much the same manner as the weeds run rampant through the flower garden and destroy by their victory the heroine's belief in the possibility of the beautiful. As in "The Friend of the Family," marriage, which should bring fulfillment, results instead in stultification. Even the comfort that Margaret Sargent can take in her continuing ability to see the truth is denied the heroine of "The Weeds," to whom is granted only the recognition of how easy it is to tell an untruth.

VII   A Meeting Ground

Without question, the most persistent emphasis in *The Company She Keeps* is on Margaret Sargent who, in many ways, is similar to the women James Agee has described.[21] Like them, she is caught in the dilemma of trying to sustain the "uneasy egocentricity" brought about by her new freedom. Margaret, too, vacillates between "wanting marriage and avoiding it." And she, too, has been "hurt and dulled by the fractures and foulnesses" of her experiences. Her situation is, indeed, paradoxical: the honesty that she values so highly does not allow her to gloss over her weaknesses, which she views with irrational harshness as the result of her intense self-preoccupation; and her grossly magnified weaknesses do not make it possible for her to be as "good" as she would wish. Because she does not live up to her own high standards, she debases her own worth. But by not loving herself, she is unable to love anyone else. And society offers no solution. Instead, the company she has elected to keep simply adds to her sense of unease.

In "The Man in the Brooks Brothers Shirt," Mary McCarthy

describes Margaret Sargent's disenchantment with the life she has chosen and her awareness of the gradual diminishing of "a feeling of uniqueness and identity, a feeling she had once had when, at twenty, she had come to New York and had her first article accepted by a liberal weekly, but which had slowly been rubbed away by four years of being on the inside of the world that had looked magic from Portland, Oregon." As this passage indicates, the disillusionment that Margaret experiences is the result of the discrepancy that exists between reality and expectation.

This recognition acts as a unifying theme in *The Company She Keeps* and in *Cast a Cold Eye*, as it does in *Memories of a Catholic Girlhood.* And, as in the autobiographical work, the irony of the animating vision creates effective dramatic tension. Not unexpectedly, in "the world that had looked magic from Portland, Oregon," marriage is not what it seems either; nor does it resemble—one can conjecture—the glamourized versions of adolescent fantasies. "Ghostly Father, I Confess," "The Weeds," and "The Friend of the Family" are depressing analyses of the failure of human relationships.

Although Mary McCarthy suggests no alternative to the world she describes (except that of a totally bourgeois existence), she does present a partial solution in "Ghostly Father, I Confess." The self-understanding provided by introspection and psychoanalysis can allow an individual to see himself with a certain amount of objective clarity, a quality admired by Mary McCarthy. Yet to know why one reacts in a certain way to a particular situation or person does not mean that one can willfully avoid acting in that manner. As Miss McCarthy admitted in the Introduction to *Theatre Chronicles,* abstract reasoning could not crush the fact of a successful play. Neither can self-knowledge and rationality repudiate an action, as the heroines of her fiction dramatize.

Mary McCarthy has said of George Bernard Shaw that his characters are paradoxes. The same observation holds true of the persons she describes in her sketches: the con man who traffics in *objets d'art*, the ingratiating Pflaumen, the Yale man, the baffling cicerone, and, of course, Margaret Sargent. Accordingly, the key that explains the figure assumes most often the form of a discovery concerning what is apparently a contradiction in the nature of the character: what there is about the inner man that exists in contradistinction to his outward appearance. As Miss McCarthy has observed, a paradox is eternal. This observation explains the inconclusiveness of her own stories which end, in the main, not with a resolution but with a revelation. This same inconclusiveness attests to her intention to create characters who are immortal, that is, comic characters who exist as objects.

Very obviously, Miss McCarthy writes from experience. And her field of vision *is* narrow. But by allowing her definition of focus, this narrowness is her strength as well as her weakness. In *The Oasis* and in *The Groves of Academe,* she accepts as limits the "world" of the modern intellectual. In these later works, however, she discards her autobiographical heroine and experiments with different voices. But behind the various masks that she affects is the irony implicit in the awareness that not only are things (including intellectuals) not what they seem but that knowledge is no insurance that man will change the foolishness of his ways.

CHAPTER 5

The Tree of Thought

A S POINTED OUT in the previous chapter, Mary McCarthy "sees" generically as well as particularly. This ability to look beyond (and beneath) the immediate object works to her advantage as a satirist. But in her longer fiction she restricts rather sharply the categories that her major characters represent. In *The Company She Keeps* and in *Cast a Cold Eye*, the fictional personages are assembled from various areas of life—almost randomly it seems; but in *The Oasis* (1949) and in *The Groves of Academe* (1952), the central characters can be labeled with reasonable accuracy as "intellectuals." In *A Charmed Life* (1955), the scope broadens again to include the assorted inhabitants of an artists' colony, only a few of whom are intellectuals, and then narrows once more to discuss nine graduates of Vassar College in *The Group* (1963).

Integral to the satirical writing of Mary McCarthy is a concern not only with characters who are both singular and representative of a category but also with the category itself and the customs and institutions native to it. What allows her to direct her satire against categories as well as individuals is the exclusiveness of her vision. In *The Groves of Academe*, for example, by concentrating on only the members of the faculty of Jocelyn College, she portrays the liberal college through their constant talk and maneuverings. To turn Addison's words about, she succeeds in charging "whole armies" while gunning simultaneously the "single foe" *and* the military as a category in one carefully launched offensive.

Also, by writing about what she knows, Miss McCarthy has the "facts" of her world at her disposal. She is aware of corners where pretension can hide and cupboards where useless doctrines have accumulated. And she delights in giving the room an airing, in sweeping out what has been swept under the rug. In *The Anatomy of Satire,* Gilbert Highet points out that "in the work of the finest satirists there is the minimum of convention, the maximum of reality."[1] The subject matter of satire, he states, "is always concrete, usually topical, often personal. It deals with actual cases, mentions real people by name or describes them unmistakably (and often unflatteringly), talks of this moment and this city, and this special, very recent, very fresh deposit of corruption whose stench is still in the satirist's curling nostrils" (16). While pretending "to be a photograph," the satire that deals with the inhabitants of this world should "in fact be a caricature" (190).

Mary McCarthy's knowledge of what she is satirizing allows her to effect this kind of "realism"—to play with surfaces convincingly; to reproduce externals that have an appearance of verisimilitude; in short, to give the reader a photograph that is really a caricature, a distortion of reality. But the distortion is necessary if the satirist is to call attention to the object of attack— if he is to succeed in forcing the reader to see what is wrong with the familiar objects that compose the reader's world.

In *Memories of a Catholic Girlhood* and in *The Company She Keeps,* it is apparent that Mary McCarthy tries to view herself very honestly. In her longer fiction, a similar honesty is evident. But while Margaret Sargent turned her gaze inward, Miss McCarthy in the satirical novels, having discarded her autobiographical heroine, turns her gaze outward. The soul-searching of Margaret Sargent becomes an exploration of the nature of a habitat. As Margaret Sargent's honesty made her want to expose the shortcomings that prevented her from being as good as she would like to be, Mary McCarthy's honesty causes her to expose what is wrong with her chosen environment.

Limiting the effectiveness of Miss McCarthy's satire, however, is a basic sympathy stemming from identification with and participation in what she ridicules. At the conclusion of *The Groves of Academe,* Henry Mulcahy answers a question by quoting the paradox of the liar: "A Cretin says, all Cretins are liars." A similar reflexivity is embedded in the writing of Mary McCarthy: Vassar girls, particularly those of the class of 1933, are somewhat ridiculous; an artists' colony contains in it morally destructive elements that war against integrity and ambition; a progressive college finds itself trapped by the liberalism it espouses; and a utopian colony and the assorted ideals that provide its reason for being collapse because intellectuals will insist on being intellectuals (i.e., people). Whether Miss McCarthy's honesty is strong enough to override the pernicious effects of an identification which is basically sympathetic becomes a critical issue of major importance in determining the effectiveness of her satire.

In "Characters in Fiction" Mary McCarthy finds fault with the device of narrative mimicry that she uses in such a work as *The Groves of Academe*: "The reader, tuned in, is left in no doubt as to where he is physically, and yet in many of these books he finds himself puzzled by the very vocal consciousness he has entered: is it good or bad, impartial or biased? Can it be trusted as Huck Finn or Marcel or David Copperfield could be trusted?" As she has indicated in this essay, the author cannot possibly step outside his characters to make upright their crooked vision. Neither can he speak through an alter ego. The reader is therefore left holding tenuously to whatever revelation has befallen the fictional character.

But some degree of authorial responsibility is important to good satire. Ridicule of any sort suggests a wrongness in the object of derision. Imperfection, in turn, implies the possibility of perfection, that is, rightness. A satire, therefore, suggests that the author considers what he ridicules as being either grandly or superficially flawed. Although a work of satire rarely offers a manifesto outlining a method of reform, the attitude of the author to his material does imply, usually, what he considers right in contradistinction to what he has exposed as wrong. But if the attitude of the author cannot be determined because (as in *The Groves of Academe*) the author has gone to great lengths to hide his own attitudes, then the effectiveness of the satire is vitiated in a way that goes beyond the problem of ridicule against objects with which the satirist shares a sympathetic identification. If the "wrong" that the satirist has revealed is to be balanced and thus to be evaluated properly, the "right" that exists in the world beyond that of the satire must be supplied by the reader when the author's "voice" is missing. If the values of the reader approximate those of the author, all is well and good. When they do not, the reader fails to see the disillusion behind the immediate work and becomes convinced that the satirist is only negative—as certain critics consider Miss McCarthy to be—and therefore untrustworthy. Or even worse, the reader believes that he is reading a realistic piece of fiction; and, instead of recognizing the faults that the satirist has held up to ridicule, he sympathizes with the mistaken attitudes and warped institutions.

Discounting ethical considerations (arising from the kind of self-satire that Miss McCarthy writes) and putting aside momentarily esthetic difficulties (resulting from the device of narrative mimicry and the shortening of distance), the identification of Mary McCarthy with what she satirizes suggests that the fault lies not with the way of life considered as a whole but either *within* that way of life or *without* as a weakness built into the generic animal—man. Ruled out and unnecessary are any suggestions having to do with a completely different manner of living. Certainly, one supposes, Miss McCarthy need not have joined forces and then stayed with the intellectuals if they are such a shallow bunch of trimmers as she makes them out to be. The implication is that she has chosen the best there is; but, because she does see what is wrong with the way of life that she has elected, she despairs. And, since she has a fine sense of the comic, she turns that despair into satire.

These observations verge very closely on being a statement about the purpose of satire. To assume blandly, as many critics have done, that all satire seeks to reform is an oversimplification. What must be recognized is that satire is primarily a literary genre, a form of artistic expression. The force that drives the satirist and shapes his material is his vision as an artist, a vision that makes him temperamentally unable to accept the evils that he sees and that causes him to describe them in the manner characteristic to satire: through such devices as exaggeration, irony, antithesis, and parody, among others. Mary McCarthy's satire is successful to the degree that it lets the reader see what is wrong with man and certain of his institutions; and it is ineffective in that it does not make clear what standards these institutions fail to meet or what virtues man fails to exemplify. Her satire is *not* unsuccessful because it does not suggest a "cure."

"The tree of life is greener than the tree of thought," Miss

McCarthy has said, quoting Hegel. Yet *The Oasis* and *The Groves of Academe* are the result of her intellectual vision. She does not make the reader sympathize with her characters because to do so would lessen the effect of her satire. And she keeps most of her characters in the category of "objects" so as to reveal what is comic about their actions and attitudes. Her focus on groups helps achieve the objectivity her esthetic theory requires. The communities of intellectuals that she describes in *The Oasis* and *The Groves of Academe* are held together by impartial forces—the ideals governing a utopian colony or a cohesiveness that results from belonging to the faculty of a college. Mary McCarthy does not concern herself with, as Faulkner has said, "the old fierce pull of blood" that binds one member of a family, even against his will, to the others. Accordingly, even though Mary McCarthy writes from "life," in the translation of experience into art, the ideas and talk in *The Oasis* and *The Groves of Academe* outweigh feelings and actions.

I   *The Machinations of a Utopia*

The members of a utopian colony form a collective protagonist in *The Oasis* (1949). The action takes place in the late spring and early summer in the year of 1946 or 1947, but the events are not those of contemporary history. This particular oasis is being established as a refuge from a world that is moving quickly and definitely toward a third world war. Miss McCarthy has pointed out that "a novel cannot be laid in the future, since the future, until it happens, is outside the order of nature; no prophecy or cautionary tale like *1984* is a novel."[2] Elsewhere she describes *The Oasis* as "a *conte*, a *conte philosophique*."[3]

This work, then, must be examined on its own terms—as a philosophical *tale* and not a *roman philosophique*, as Cyril Connolly describes it. *The Oasis* is a form of "let's pretend." Taking X group of intellectuals from the known milieu of Y, Miss McCarthy places them in the imaginary setting of Z. Reasoning from her knowledge of how X comport themselves in Y, she conjectures how X will act in Z. To add interest, she posits that Z is a utopian colony that is similar in some respects to Brook Farm. But the emphasis in this work is less on Z than on X. Miss McCarthy is trying to show the *effect* of this experiment in utopian living on the colonists and is not attempting to prescribe a panacea for the world's economic and political ills. Thus, *The Oasis* is not a utopian tale but a *conte philosophique* about a utopia.

Conceived and written during the years immediately following World War II, *The Oasis* stands as a document to a political mood. ". . . Even Koestler was writing at that period about the possibility of founding oases—that's where I took the title. . . . It seemed possible still, utopian but possible, to change the world on a small scale. Everyone was trying to live in a very principled way, but with quite a lot of energy, the energy that peace had brought, really."[4] Then, as she writes, "the Russians got the atom bomb, and the hydrogen bomb came. That was the end of *any* hope, or at least any hope that I can see of anything being done except in a massive way."[5] Hydrogen warfare, she says in a later essay, by permitting the survival of neither civilization nor faith, negates the possibilities of objectives apart from the holocaust of war itself. "If we die, it will not be for freedom but out of a kind of inert necessity, in a chain reaction of challenge-and-response like the process of fission itself."[6]

With ironic suitability, Miss McCarthy has her urban, rootless people set up housekeeping on a mountaintop cut off from the metropolitan civilization that has sustained them and given them what tradition they possess. On this intellectual Olympus, the men attempt to act like gods, setting up their own rules and systems of value and meting out justice to one another in an arbitrarily principled fashion. The chief members of the colony are drawn from persons with whom Miss McCarthy has associated in real life. Brock Brower writes: "In *The Oasis*, she might as *well* have used the real names, her Utopian colony was so patently inhabited by all her old soul mates from the Europe-America Groups (organized to help refugee intellectuals in the Forties) and so raucous with their chivvying, backbiting quarrels."[7]

Mary McCarthy, however, has denied the importance of autobiography in this work. Everything written since *The Company She Keeps,* she maintains, despite autobiographical elements, "has been conceived as a fiction, even a thing like *The Oasis,* that's supposed to have all these real people in it. The whole story is a complete fiction. Nothing of the kind ever happened; after all, it happens in the future."[8] And pointing out the similarities between Dwight Macdonald and Macdougal Macdermott or between Will Taub and Philip Rahv gets nowhere. The characters do exist in her fiction as realizable people in their own right.

Although Miss McCarthy admits that she leaves herself open for readers to play the *roman à clef* game, she objects to this kind of detective work on the esthetic grounds that it deflects attention from the fiction. "What I really do is take real plums and put them in an imaginary cake. If you're interested in the cake, you get rather annoyed with people saying what species the real plum was."[9] The "imaginary cake," then, is the colony itself. And it is the colony collectively that Mary McCarthy is satirizing. Intellectuals, she is saying, talk too much, and as a group they suffer from an occupational inability to put theory into practice.

In *The Oasis,* the thinking man's paradise comes equipped with a ready-built, but somewhat antiquated, abandoned summer hotel. Founded in accordance with the precepts of an Italian anarchist believed by the utopians to be hiding somewhere in Europe, the colony is supposed to set an example for "a network of autonomous, cooperative communities with unlimited freedom for the individual. . . ."[10] What unites the colonists, most of whom are disenchanted liberals, is their lack of faith in any form of centralized bureaucracy. But from the beginning, the oasis is rife with quarrels and two distinct groups quickly emerge—the purists and the realists. Led by Macdougal Macdermott, the purists believe in the perfectibility of mankind; the realists, commanded by Will Taub, scoff at this assumption as naïve. "To them Utopia was justified on sheerly practical grounds, as a retreat from atomic warfare, a summer-vacation colony, a novelty in personal relations; and though in their hearts they too hoped for some millennial outcome of the experiment, for the reign of justice and happiness, they shrank from a definition of the colony which committed them to any positive belief."[11]

Between these two factions is "an assortment of persons of diffuse and uncommitted good will" that includes, among others, two editors of a news weekly, a Latin teacher, a Protestant minister, an unemployed World War II veteran, an alcoholic woman illustrator, a middle-aged poet, and several New York high school teachers (142). All share, however, a belief in utopia as "the right to a human existence" and a conviction that conditions in the outside world are not conducive to such an existence.

Although none is gullible enough to believe that he can turn back the clock absolutely, each respects the Founder's idea of *limit*: "Agreeing, in principle, that the machine was to be distrusted, they had nevertheless voted to use in their experiment the bicycle, the carpet-sweeper, and the sewing-machine, any machine, in fact, to which a man contributed his own proportionate share of exertion and which tired him like the plough or the hoe" (144). The absence of an electric power plant precipitates the first of the crises that advance the "plot" of *The Oasis*.

Joe Lockman (Joe Loucheim in the text as it appears in *Horizon*) causes the initial upset by accidentally flooding the wood stove with kerosene so that Katy Norell, assigned to cook the colonists' breakfast, burns her eyebrows and bangs. This gaucherie is the first action that sets Joe apart from the rest of the utopians. If a contrary positive principle does exist in this work, Joe Lockman, a self-made businessman and clearly not an intellectual, embodies that counter force. But Joe is not an attractive figure, for his zealous optimism and glad-handed gregariousness isolate him from the other members and make him seem simple by contrast. He is not a person temperamentally or intellectually able to save mankind.

The second crisis is a more important one, for it forces the somewhat ill-defined realist camp to act as a group and to take a firm stand against the purists. Early the first evening, Joe had made the mistake of "scaring" Will Taub by coming up behind the realist leader with a gun and pretending to capture Taub. As a result of this affront to Taub and the incident involving the flooded stove, the realists find Joe too different from themselves and create the second juncture by calling a meeting to try to oust him from the colony. They fail because of the good humor of Macdermott, who makes their seriousness about such trivial offenses appear ridiculous. Joe is allowed to stay, and the issue is dropped. The resolution of this skirmish, by uniting both realists and purists in a spirit of greater tolerance, marks the "beginning of the lyrical phase of the community." On the practical side, however, the purists seem to have secured the advantage.

But, as in the short stories, the substance of *The Oasis* derives from the exact and penetrating analyses of the various colonists. The crises are merely intrusions that allow the colonists to react in their varying ways and foreshadow the ultimate failure of utopia by showing the fallaciousness of the purists' belief in perfectibility. These crises, spurred usually by some physical circumstance, quickly become intellectualized, so that the actual events, like the colonists themselves, act as representatives of various principles.

After the second crisis, the purists, although hopeful that the failure of the realists to codify their beliefs would bring about their downfall, are conscious that they are gradually abandoning their own principles in favor of simply getting along with Taub and his faction on a live-and-let-live basis. "The discovery that one cannot convince an opponent and that it is hopeless to go on trying involves a confession of subjectivity that deprives the world of meaning: the colony, it seemed to the Norells and Leo Raphael, a poet, was losing its *raison d'être* . . ." (179). The realists, however, remain unregenerate and refuse to acknowledge past or present guilt; they treat the colony as an exceptional case that, by its estrangement from the rest of the world, can prove nothing to that world.

The sense that the oasis is separated from the real world and not relevant to it causes the third crisis. This comes about when a letter from their founder, reaffirming the worth of small, peripheral communities like their own, creates an awareness of their selfishness. Katy Norell, who speaks most often for Miss McCarthy, reflects that by neglecting to spread the gospel of their success and "by becoming merely self-subsistent," they had failed the founder. ". . . The others, however saddened or thoughtful, felt no impulse to join her in a *Domine non sum dignus* ["Lord, I am not worthy"] which, for all its sincerity, had so clearly personal a reference; she was comparing herself, with all her shortcomings and weaknesses, to the great work the letter suggested to her" (182). But as more letters from Monteverdi arrive, informing them that what little news of the colony had filtered to Europe had created a favorable response in those countries not yet under Communist rule, the other colonists begin to share her despair.

Accordingly, at a general meeting held on the Fourth of July,

Leo Raphael goads the colonists into action. His enthusiasm immediately inflames his audience with a desire to do something constructive toward realizing their goals and breaking away from their isolation. Plans for sending a peace fleet to Europe to transport those Europeans who wish to join their movement are hazily advanced. The utopians volunteer to put out a pamphlet, to write to congressmen, to get articles in leading magazines, and to convince college presidents of the worth of their scheme. This enthusiasm precipitates the actual crisis. For, when faced with putting their ideas into action, the colonists back down, each finding reasons not to carry out his particular part of Operation Peace. It is then that the utopians realize that their escape from the outer world has truly been an estrangement. By renouncing the world, they have cut off former ties and rendered themselves unable to communicate with acquaintances and employers from their past life. A kind of sullen uneasiness settles on the colonists, broken by the irrepressible Joe who announces a fireworks display that allows the colonists to call for adjournment. The only semi-practical result of the meeting and Operation Peace is the agreement to adopt one of the least ambitious of the various schemes—that Macdermott write a pamphlet outlining Leo's plan.

The fourth and final crisis follows the next day when a celebration picnic takes place. The colonists had agreed to spend the morning picking the small wild strawberries in the woods and then to meet in the meadow for a picnic and the awarding of a prize to the person with the fullest basket. But half-way through the morning, plans go awry when Will Taub and his wife discover in the meadow three strangers who are picking the wild berries "where they grew in the greatest abundance, and with the sun-warmed flavor of wine." Taub refuses to speak to the three berry pickers, and his wife's gentle attempts to get their attention fail. Disgruntled, the Taubs return to the main house where they tell Katy Norell and Eleanor Macdermott about the intruders. The men being absent, Katy goes out alone and tries to reason politely with the three invaders who, after listening to her explanation, continue with their picking. Returning to the main house, she finds that a quarrel is taking place. "The young people . . . were defending Katy's action, while the older members were furiously condemning her for individualistic conduct. No principles were being invoked . . ." (200-1). Angry at the hostility being directed toward his wife, Preston defends her by taking it upon himself to rout the unwanted trio. The young veteran follows him, bringing along Joe Lockman's gun. Unaware that the gun is loaded only with blanks, the intruders respond to the threat of violence and leave after a short interval.

The debate that follows this event makes the colonists realize that their "victory" is really a defeat in that several of their cherished principles had been sacrificed. What this incident shows is that theory, when put to the test of reality, is inadequate. Katy, her husband, and the young veteran acted individualistically and intuitively by resorting to force in order to defend the utopians' rights of legal possession; but their instinctive responses betrayed them by being antithetic to the basic premise of the colony and, therefore, to the colonists' professed beliefs. The incident reveals irrefutably the fallacy of the purists' assumption that by changing their social environment they could change themselves. If they could not as individuals change, then the hope that they could look forward to some moral transformation as a group similarly was doomed. Each knows that a phase of the colony had ended: ". . . something had been lost that was perhaps an essential ingredient—a man can live without self-respect, but a group goes to pieces, demoralized by the ugliness it sees reflected in itself" (206).

Following the picnic lunch Katy and Taub talk. And it is after this discussion that Katy acknowledges that her own "hunger for goodness was an appetency not of this world and not to be satisfied by actions, which would forever cheat its insistencies." Even "the desire to *embody* virtue appeared a shallow and vulgar craving, the refracted error of a naïve and acquisitive culture which imagined that there was nothing—beauty, honor, title of nobility, charm, youth, happiness—which persistency could not secure" (211). She conjectures further that the utopia would fail completely unless the colonists put their energies into marketing a tangible, such as cheese or wine, instead of an intangible like a political ideology or a morality.

Lulled by the wine she has drunk and by her new awareness and sense of limitation, Katy lies back on the grass. A scene from the future intrudes on her consciousness. She sees in her vision the defection of one of the colonists, Jim Haines, the representative of the ordinary man, eluding the grasp of the theoretician to return to former ways. She envisions Joe Lockman—still a part of the colony, but soon to leave, to go onto new ventures—as having tarried briefly in this one and having gained nothing. While she is trying to count on her fingers those colonists who would remain, she falls asleep. With this dream *The Oasis* ends. Human nature remains a constant; utopia is, after all, only a vision.

In "The Fact in Fiction," Mary McCarthy has noted that institutions are prone to scandal: "they attempt to keep the news in, contain it, and in doing so they magnify it, and then, as people say, 'the lid is off.' "[12] The isolation of the utopia provides an atmosphere similar to that of an institution. Accordingly, the admittedly trivial incidents that comprise the plot of *The Oasis* get blown up many times greater than their actual weight and size. Although this distortion is comic, it is the reader's simultaneous awareness of the actual pettiness of the different crises that reveals the pretentiousness of the dream and shows how weak the man with principles really is. When put to the test, the colonists' moral aversion to violence and to the tenets of the capitalistic economy is of little use. These are negative assumptions that do not constitute a cohesive way of life. If the colonists had been of one mind, however, they could perhaps have put together a set of "house rules" that would have prescribed what action to take against such an event as the unwanted strawberry pickers. But this is one of the dilemmas of *The Oasis*: the colonists are divided among themselves. Like the artist, the intellectual is an outsider and, consequently, somewhat anti-social in his behavior. *The Oasis* is a dramatization of this premise.

Although Mary McCarthy describes well the larger issues and principles at stake behind the seeming minutiae of the actual "crises," the portraits (or caricatures, as the case may be) of the colonists give this tale what life it possesses. As in the short stories, the singularity of the characters is also what makes them representatives of a general class. Within the general class of intellectuals, however, a few sub-genres can be detected, for example, Macdermott the pacifist, and Taub the cynic. Although these portraits are stylized, the artificiality of the stylization allows Mary McCarthy to dissect her characters and their varying attitudes wittily and precisely. Consequently, amid the silliness-seriousness of the squabbles, some of the characters stand out rather vividly, so that the reader becomes interested in them as people who have emotions and not merely as puppets capable only of mouthing certain ideas. For example, Katy Norell becomes convincing as a human being (and as a Mary McCarthy heroine) who voices a very human feeling when she acknowledges the impracticality of her ideals. Joe Lockman engenders some degree of sympathy because he is so plainly out of his element in the rarefied air of the mountaintop. And certainly Will Taub is complexly interesting as an antagonist.

Accordingly, the satire against intellectuals and against what happens when intellectuals band together becomes diluted. This weakening seems inevitable, however, for the satire in *The Oasis* is directed in part against those hopes that Mary McCarthy once shared. Thus the ideals are not so amiss as are the persons who hold them and the way they put them into practice. And a single individual *is* invariably more interesting than a collection of individuals held up for examination as a group. As the emphasis in this tale is put increasingly on the different colonists—with the analysis at times plunging below satire and beyond topicality— the satire against the oasis becomes lessened until, at the end, Miss McCarthy is content to rest her case on Katy Norell's reflections which, in essence, embrace the philosophical position of the realists and on the general observation that men are foolish to suppose that they can change their ways by changing their environment. In "The Weeds," Miss McCarthy wrote, ". . . for everything returns to itself and a marriage made out of loneliness and despair will be lonely and desperate."[13] The utopians can return only to themselves, and for some the limitations of the self are discouragingly severe.

II   *The Machinations of a "Progressive" College*

The Groves of Academe is a satirical treatment of another kind of utopia—an experimental college. Like the oasis, the closed and structured society of the college offers Miss McCarthy a "world within a world." And, like the utopians, the Jocelyn faculty, by acting in accord with the values appropriate to its milieu, behaves oddly when judged against external standards.

Critics have tried to find echoes of Bard and Sarah Lawrence in the fictional Jocelyn, and Miss McCarthy admits that the college she invented, although not at all like Sarah Lawrence or

Bennington, is quite a bit like Bard. But, she explains, "I really wanted to make a weird imaginary college of my own."[14] She succeeds well; Jocelyn *is* "weird," and, as a representative of a progressive college, somewhat unrepresentative. But, since *The Groves of Academe* ridicules not simply the idea of an experimental college but the pretentiousness of "higher" education in general, an exact correspondence between the fictional Jocelyn and a "real" college is unnecessary. All that is necessary is that Jocelyn must be believable as a center of learning in contemporary America. And, despite much witty exaggeration, the "weird, imaginary college" invented by Mary McCarthy does succeed in providing a plausible environment. Planned "to strike a middle course between the existing extremes, between Aquinas and Dewey, the modern dance and the labor movement," Jocelyn wished its students "neither to till the soil as at Antioch nor weave on looms as at Black Mountain; they were to be grounded neither in the grass-roots present as at Sarah Lawrence nor in the great-books past as at St. John's or Chicago; they were to specialize neither in verse-writing, nor in the poetic theatre, nor in the techniques of co-operative living—they were simply to be free, spontaneous, and co-educational."[15]

Satirizing Jocelyn College was undoubtedly child's play to Mary McCarthy. All she had to do was stop, look, listen, remember . . . and exaggerate. But Henry Mulcahy was another matter. Making *him* believable involved a complexity of problems. Miss McCarthy has explained that the idea of *The Groves of Academe* presented itself first "as a plot with a single character at the center."[16] The single character is Henry Mulcahy, and the plot is "his campaign for justice. Justice, both in quotes, you know, and serious in a way. What *is* justice for the unemployable person?"[17] The beginning (Mulcahy's dismissal) and the ending (his triumph over the president of the college) were thought out before the middle was imagined: "I didn't see exactly what would happen in between. . . . But I did see that there would be his campaign for reinstatement and then his secret would be discovered. In this case that he had *not* been a Communist."[18]

In "The Contagion of Ideas" (Summer, 1952), Miss McCarthy discusses the issue of Communism and "the right to teach"; and she mentions the curious advantages of party membership in certain academic circles. In *The Groves of Academe,* she dramatizes this concept by making Mulcahy base his "campaign for justice" on the vulnerability of Maynard Hoar. Mulcahy feigns prior party membership, knowing that Hoar, as president of Jocelyn, cannot risk being exposed as an anti-liberal and a hypocrite for having fired one of his faculty on the grounds of Communist Party affiliation.

Miss McCarthy states that she had no desire to write *The Groves of Academe* from a consciousness other than Mulcahy's. ". . . To me, the interest lay in trying to see it from the professor's point of view and mouthing it in the clichés and the hissing jargon of his vocabulary."[19] Although she found pretending to be a vindictive male professor somewhat exhilarating, the undertaking, she admits, was basically dishonest. No mere feat of the imagination would ever let her know what it felt like to be such a bizarre individual. But an added incentive to this game of make-believe was her conviction that if she could understand Mulcahy she would have a key to such demagogic figures as Hitler. "To do this, naturally, I had to use every bit of Mulcahy there was in me, and there was not very much: I am not a paranoid, nor a liar, nor consumed with hatred, nor a man, for that matter. But this very fact was the stimulus."[20]

The distortion in *The Groves of Academe* is, therefore, threefold. First, the reader must see the world largely in terms of Mulcahy's warped vision and believe in that projection. Second, he must recognize that Jocelyn and environs have already been distorted by Miss McCarthy's satiric intent. And third, he must look at a world that in actuality *is* somewhat distorted. The atypical tutorial system of Jocelyn allows the faculty members a closeness to their students that is unusual in an American college. Likewise, in the liberal atmosphere fostered by the ideology of the experimental college, Mulcahy's alleged Communist Party membership works in his favor instead of against him. Mulcahy is aware of this element of fantasy in Jocelyn and the inversion of certain values, and he puts to his own devious use "the freakish character of its tides of opinion, the anomalies of its personnel, the madness of its methodology . . ." (90).

In a sense, Mulcahy is a stock figure in an academic novel, one who can claim kinship with "the ugly dialectician, the parasitic philosopher-poet at the gentleman's banquet, the vice-ridden master, the learned unsavory monk, the Socrates-Falstaff-ghetto-intellectual. With all his personal grossness and labyrinthine wit, this ugly-wise one appears as both the idol and the outcast of the genteel academy, the topsy-turvy king of polite cultivation."[21] Mary McCarthy's description of Mulcahy links him to this intellectual archetype. "A tall, soft-bellied, lisping man with a tense, mushroom-white face, rimless bifocals, and graying thin red hair, he was intermittently aware of a quality of personal unattractiveness that emanated from him like a miasma; this made him self-pitying, uxorious, and addicted also to self-love, for he associated it with his destiny as a portent of some personal epiphany" (13). A Joycean scholar, he identifies himself with the martyrs of modern literary history—Joyce, Kafka, and Proust; with Joyce's protagonists, Bloom and Earwicker; and, of course, with Jesus Christ. Not surprisingly, when he devises his plan for reinstatement he chooses to parade in the clothes of a political martyr—a victim of the House Un-American Activities Committee witch hunts and of Maynard Hoar.

The epigraph from Horace, *Atque inter silvas academi quaerere verum* (and to search for truth amidst the groves of Academus) is, of course, ironic. For the concern of the novel is with Mulcahy's endeavors to abuse the truth. His strategy is many-faceted as a result of a talent for self-dramatization—an ability that he shares with Miss McCarthy—which allows him to see on many levels at once and to visualize results of diverse courses of action. After the abating of his first flush of annoyance at the letter of dismissal, he decides to approach Hoar privately through faculty petition rather than to threaten the president with exposure as an anti-liberal before the American Association of University Professors Grievance Committee. Involvement with the A.A.U.P., he reasons, might entail an investigation and the resultant disclosure of the falsity of his alleged Communism. Next, he determines to use his wife and children to enlist faculty sympathies, and he invents a heart condition for Cathy. Convincing himself that the news of his dismissal would kill his wife, he imagines immediately the pathetic appeal of four motherless children.

Mulcahy, it must be noted, after a brief moment of recognizing that he is inventing, *believes* his own fantasies. In his eyes, a mark of his genius lies in his ability to take from "the usual disjunct fragments of personal experience a persuasive whole which had a figurative truth more impressive than the data of reality, and hence . . . truer in the final analysis, more universal in Aristotle's sense" (88). To scheme so elaborately is to him an indication of brilliance: ". . . he was the first, the very first, so far as he knew, in all history to expose the existence of a frame-up by framing himself first" (89). His firm conviction of superiority to other men lies at the root of his paranoia. For he believes himself envied, maligned, and persecuted by his intellectual inferiors.

His next step is to approach the faculty. Instinct prompts him to appeal first to Domna Rejnev. Miss McCarthy speaks most often in *The Groves of Academe* through this well-bred, highly intelligent Russian girl. At twenty-three, Domna, a Radcliffe graduate, teaches Russian literature and French at Jocelyn. Similar in many respects to a Turgenev heroine, she appears to stifle in surroundings that are conventional: ". . . her finely cut, mobile nostrils quivered during a banal conversation as though, literally, seeking air. . . . She had a severe, beautiful, clear-cut profile, very pure ivory skin. . . . Her very beauty had the quality, not of radiance or softness, but of incorruptibility; it was the beauty of an absolute or a political theorem" (39). Only her eyes, which are "grey and queerly lit from within, as by some dangerous electricity," hint at a passionate intensity behind her seeming calmness and restraint. Mulcahy had spotted her instantly as someone to cultivate as a friend, and he had estimated her from the beginning as a girl "who could very easily throw herself away" (40). Consequently, he takes full advantage of Domna's passion for justice and her fondness for Cathy and unburdens his "soul," describing with a storyteller's concern for details the circumstances of his wife's imaginary illness. Dramatically, he emphasizes how Cathy must be spared the ugly news of his unjust dismissal, and suddenly, without warning, he begins to weep. The "utter misery of his situation had sprung on him . . . from cover, like an animal at the throat," and he cried "hopelessly from sheer hatred of the universe, including the girl who was watching him . . ." (45).

The scheme devised by Mulcahy works out roughly as he anticipated. In fact, much of what is comic about this novel stems from the predictability of the characters and from the rapidity with which a trivial issue becomes a matter of great importance. Mulcahy proves himself adept at judging both the proclivity of institutions to foster gossip and the fondness of intellectuals to champion causes in the name of justice. For the campus is soon rife with news of his dismissal as groups of two or three faculty members gather to discuss the issue. Even the students, Mulcahy learns, are circulating a petition in his support. But at a general meeting of the literature faculty, Howard Furness, the chairman of that department, refuses to accept Mulcahy's Communist Party membership as the reason for his dismissal and declines to back the man on the grounds of his deficiencies as an instructor.

Disappointed at the failure of the department to achieve unanimity, Alma Fortune announces her resignation, a gesture which Mulcahy interprets later as a bid to share his martyr's place. Another meeting results in John Bentkoop, from Comparative Religion, and Domna forming a deputation to confront Maynard Hoar to petition for Mulcahy's reinstatement. But, like Furness, the president refuses to believe in Mulcahy's allegation of Communist Party membership. In addition, he refutes any knowledge of Cathy's illness and denies another of Mulcahy's "claims"—an informal agreement that he was to have been hired for a minimum of two years. What impresses Hoar, however, is the evidence of strong faculty backing for Mulcahy's worth as a teacher.

Unexpectedly, events turn against Mulcahy when later that day Domna discovers that not only does Cathy know of her husband's dismissal but that her "illness" is a figment of Mulcahy's imagination. Confused, the Russian girl confides in John Bentkoop and his wife, and the three young people discuss Mulcahy far into the night, deciding, of course, that they cannot reveal the fraud of Cathy's illness. For some time after, the Mulcahy issue lies dormant. Then, in February, his contract is renewed. And, as one of the chapter headings indicates, "Mulcahy Finds a Disciple." Soon Mulcahy and his new friend, Herbert Ellison, another member of the English faculty, move the novel to its climax by way of the poetry conference, of which they form a committee of two.

Like the news of his "unjust" dismissal, the conference quickly becomes a matter of considerable importance, and in a short time rumors fly about the campus concerning its purpose. Basically, all the gossip agrees only that the conference would not be representative and that it veiled some questionable ulterior motive. ". . . It was said that Mulcahy and Ellison were planning to use the symposium for an attack on contemporary verse, on formlessness, on 'pure' poetry, on 'impure,' i.e., paraphrasable, poetry, on the idea of progress, on progressive education" (196). As a result, another departmental meeting takes place, and Mulcahy and Ellison agree to make the membership of their panel more equitable.

In an unexpected way, the convening of the poets supplies Mulcahy with ammunition to use against Maynard Hoar; but, in turn, the conference manages in an equally strange fashion to renew Hoar's confidence in himself. Overhearing one of the poets, Vincent Keogh, reminisce with Mulcahy about Brooklyn College, the old days, and the John Reed Club, Hoar assumes immediately that Mulcahy's confession of Communist ties is true. With Furness' support, he questions Keogh in private the next morning. Keogh admits to having tried to interest Mulcahy in the party but states that his attempts had been unsuccessful. Mulcahy, he explains, is "one of those birds that are more Communist than the Communists in theory, but you'll never meet them on the picket-line. A weird, isolated figure, with a talent for self-dramatization . . .'" (246).

Later, believing that he has talked out of turn to the president, Keogh tells Mulcahy about the meeting and the questions that Hoar had asked. This information puts Mulcahy in a position to confront Hoar and accuse him of snooping, which he does. White-faced and malevolent, he threatens to expose Hoar to the American Association of University Professors and "to every liberal magazine and newspaper in the country" as a meddler and hypocrite. Although Mulcahy's accusations are grossly distorted, they contain enough of the truth, as Hoar sadly realizes, to discredit him and to provide Mulcahy with a club to use not merely to assure his retention at Jocelyn but to advance his position.

A short time later, Hoar telephones Bentkoop and announces that he has resigned, acknowledging that as long as he remained president, Jocelyn could never rid itself of Mulcahy. He then tells Bentkoop that the talk on Virgil given by one of the poets the previous night had reawakened his interest in classicism and renewed his faith to the extent that he had concluded his interview with Mulcahy by declaiming the first line of the first Catiline oration: " '*Quo usque tandem, Catilina, abutere patientia nostra?* How far at length, O Catiline, will you abuse our patience?' At the other end of the phone, the young man signaled to his wife, who crept up and put her ear to the receiver as the President's noble voice rolled on."

And so the search for truth in the groves of academe ends on a note of decided impersonality and ambiguity. That Mary McCarthy concludes her novel by having Maynard Hoar telephone Bentkoop and repeat his earlier interview with Mulcahy introduces an unexpected distancing, a moving away from the closeness of private conversations and departmental meetings toward an impersonality suggested by the mechanicalness of the telephone. Also, having Bentkoop be the recipient of the president's call instead of Domna Rejnev diverts attention from a character who has been treated with far greater subjectivity than has Bentkoop and one, as well, who would be expected to react to Hoar's explanation. In addition, Miss McCarthy does not make clear whether Maynard Hoar's affirmation of classicism is meaningful or simply histrionic. If all along he has represented a good force (the clear and deep waters of classicism) opposed to a bad force (the muddy and snag-filled shallows of progressivism), Miss McCarthy has described her "dark horse" in an odd way. Compared with Domna, Alma Fortune, John Bentkoop, or even Mulcahy, the president appears simple and without sufficient depth and subtlety. If progressivism has fared badly (being left in the hands of persons like Mulcahy), classicism, as a means of saving humanity, appears inadequate also. But Miss McCarthy offers no judgment. Her impersonation of Mulcahy, as she has explained in "Characters in Fiction," makes it impossible for her to step in and straighten up this confusion.

But more than the ambiguity of the ending mars *The Groves of Academe* as satire. Although in bits and pieces (particularly the chapter, "Ancient History," in which Miss McCarthy summarizes the twelve-year history of Jocelyn) the satire against the experimental college is brilliantly caustic, this high level of satiric attack is not sustained. Indeed, by the conclusion, irony has replaced satire as the dominant mode, as the reader sees a professed liberal trapped by the professed liberalism of one of his faculty. But by the time Miss McCarthy has got to the conclusion, the emphasis (despite the witty treatment of the poets during the conference) has been deflected from satire to character and in particular to the bizarre person of Mulcahy.

Interest in Mulcahy weakens this novel as a satire against the progressive college in a number of ways. Obviously, the peculiarities of Mulcahy's disposition make him a liability to *any* college faculty. Neither the fault of nor the result of progressivism, he exists outside the issue of doctrine. To show the workings of the liberal college through his eyes is not only to negate some of the validity of what is revealed but to take attention away from the satire. Jocelyn becomes less interesting than the unappealing yet compelling figure of the paranoid scholar. Miss McCarthy understood that she had touched something very deep in human nature when she created Mulcahy. As noted earlier, she has acknowledged that she believed that if she were able to understand Mulcahy by *being* Mulcahy, she would have some grasp of the mystery of a Hitler or similar demagogic figures of modern society. The grotesque workings of Mulcahy's mind *do* reveal something of the mystery of the demagogue, but such a revelation lies far beyond the purpose of satire.

III *A Meeting Ground*

In *Pioneers & Caretakers*, Louis Auchincloss has observed, "One misses the point of *The Groves of Academe* if one forgets what Miss McCarthy could do with a *nonprogressive* college. There is more sympathy on her part than appears at a first reading for the poor souls struggling for a straw of consistency under the relentless badgering of Henry Mulcahy."[22] This observation holds true also of *The Oasis*. But this sympathy is at least partially responsible for what is ineffective in these two works as satires. The commitment to the objects of satire in *The Oasis* and *The Groves of Academe* is more than esthetic; it is moral. *The Groves of Academe* is less an attack on the pedagogy of progressivism than, as in *The Oasis*, an exposure of a community of intellectuals who, it turns out, share the same failings as the rest of human kind in that they are impractical, foolish, and sometimes even dangerous. Yet the colonists and the Jocelyn faculty do attempt to live by principle and by intellect; and, even if they are ridiculous on occasion, they are better, therefore, than those who do not—at least they are worthy objects of satire. By not bothering with the rest of humanity, Miss McCarthy appears to be saying so. In *A Charmed Life* and *The Group,* a similar self-satire is evident. These works, too, continue to examine both the individual and the community in which he moves. But the community is a social one and less restricted than the mountain-top utopia or the "lotus-land" of the Jocelyn campus. Addition-ally, in *A Charmed Life* and in *The Group,* Mary McCarthy follows her own advice to a greater degree than she did in *The Oasis* or *The Groves of Academe* and gives more room to the tree of life.

CHAPTER 6

A Little Learning

SOME OF THE DEFECTS that mar *The Groves of Academe* as a work of satire also impair the satirical thrust of *A Charmed Life* (1955). The New Leeds of this novel is as foolish and dangerous as Jocelyn College, and its citizens tied as securely to artistic expression as Maynard Hoar and his faculty are to the apron strings of literature and philosophy. By concentrating on Martha Sinnott, however, Mary McCarthy places greater emphasis on characterization than on attack. The reader "sees" much of the foolishness of New Leeds through Martha's eyes, just as he "saw" the weaknesses of Jocelyn College through the eyes of Henry Mulcahy; but these characters are singular and their vision untrustworthy. Although Martha is determinedly an honest person and Mulcahy blatantly dishonest, both twist premises willfully in order to arrive at conclusions in keeping with their self-images.

Moreover, neither Martha nor Mulcahy is a representative type. The portrait of Mulcahy is not a satire of *the* college professor and that of Martha Sinnott is not a satire of *the* typical resident of an "artistic" community. This atypicalness makes them ill-suited to be either objects of satire or proper vehicles for the projection of the satirist's vision. In both these novels, satire against a community and its members yields to portraiture of an idiosyncratic character whose complexity demands that irony, previously only one of the weapons of the satirical offensive, become the dominant attitude. Consequently, the intelligent and highly individualized natures of Mulcahy and Martha Sinnott provide Mary McCarthy with a partial means of getting away from the kind of commitment that satire (particularly self-satire) necessitates to the detachment that irony permits.

The first chapter of *A Charmed Life* was written as a short story and published in *The New Yorker* (October 9, 1954). Miss

McCarthy explains that when she "conceived the idea of its being a novel, I think about all I knew was that the heroine would have to die in the end." At first she thought of letting the abortion be the cause of Martha's death, but then she discarded this ending in favor of "having her drive on the correct side of the road and get killed, because in this weird place everyone is always on the wrong side of the road. But all that is really implicit in the first chapter."[1] And the first chapter, with its satiric description of New Leeds and its list of reasons why Martha and John Sinnott should have avoided returning to this "charmed" community, does foreshadow the inevitable, tragic ending. New Leeds, Miss McCarthy makes clear, is "haunted" and contains a strong element of the fairy tale; the unexpected and the catastrophic are natural to such a community.[2]

But somewhere along the line, as the novel develops through the device of narrative mimicry and as the portraits of the New Leedsians at work and at play accumulate, the emphasis on the fabulous nature of the colony is weakened. The literalness (despite the exaggeration basic to satire and a certain amount of contrivance) of the middle chapters leads the reader to expect "a realistic continuation of everything going on in a rather moderate way."[3] In the final chapter, however, everything goes haywire, and the weirdness of New Leeds reasserts itself. *A Charmed Life*, Mary McCarthy declares, is "to some extent, a symbolic story. The novel is supposed to be about doubt."[4]

I *The Machinations of an "Artistic" Community*

The first chapter of *A Charmed Life* captures vividly and succinctly the peculiarities of New Leeds. Miss McCarthy maintains that she intended to describe a "nice, ordinary, old-fashioned New England town." But a compulsion to write "on the bias" and to see "things with a sort of swerve and swoop" causes her to distort and exaggerate: "I don't know exactly how it happens. I know I don't mean it to happen."[5] And her nice old-fashioned New England town becomes a modern horror:

Everything here multiplied, like the jellyfish in the harbor. There were *three* village idiots, grinning, in the post office; the average winter resident who settled here had had three wives; there were eight young bohemians, with beards, leaning from their pickup trucks; twenty-one town drunkards. In wife-beating, child neglect, divorce, automobile accidents, falls, suicide, the town was on a sort of statistical rampage, like the highways on a holiday week end.[6]

The inhabitants lead a charmed life because some mysterious force protects them from death. "They have dozens of terrible accidents, and they're all crippled in one way or another, and yet they have this marvelous power of survival. All those drunks and human odds and ends."[7] Drinking is one of the problems that accompany living in New Leeds, and the village boasts strong chapters of the Women's Christian Temperance Union (for the locals) and of Alcoholics Anonymous (for the "foreigners"). "Martha said people came here because they wanted to become alcoholics and were looking for a Rome to do as the Romans did in." The excessive quantity of reformed or reforming alcoholics, the Sinnotts discover, takes the joy out of drinking: ". . . it was typical of New Leeds that you could not take a drink without wondering whether you might become an alcoholic. Everything here cast a menacing shadow before it, a shade of future perdition" (14).

Martha and John Sinnott settle in New Leeds, fully aware of these inherent dangers and of their own ominous qualifications for establishing residence in the community: "two tiny incomes, an obscure fame (Martha's), a free-lancing specialty (John's), and the plan of doing something original" (15). Martha differs only superficially from other Mary McCarthy heroines—Margaret Sargent in *The Company She Keeps*, the wife in "The Weeds," and Katy Norell in *The Oasis*. Highly self-critical and impatient with clumsiness and untruthfulness, she sets as a pattern of behavior an ideal standard impossible of achievement. She describes herself as " 'an absolutist. I want to be a paragon uniting all the virtues.' " Her arrogance stems from an inner uncertainty. And yet, like Margaret Sargent, Martha is intelligent, well-educated, and attractive, "a strange, poetical-looking being, with very fair, straight hair done in a little knot, a quaint oval face, very dark wide-set eyes, and a small, slight figure; she had been on the stage" (4-5). As well, she had spent three of the seven years she and John had been married studying for her doctorate in philosophy, and "three more years in which she did odd jobs—writing theatre notices, recording novels for the blind, making a

new translation of *The Wild Duck* for an off-Broadway production—and one year that was wasted in false starts on her play"
(8). The decision to move to New Leeds was prompted, in part,
by Martha's need to have a controlled amount of solitude so that
she could finish the play.

John, too, is striking looking, "tall and small-boned, with high-
coloring, neatly inscribed features, and dark-brown, stiffly curling
hair . . ." (5). Although capable of self-sacrifice and seemingly
of placing Martha's interests above his own, he is weak where
he should be strong. Because he wishes Martha to be invulner-
able or perfect, her penchant for self-criticism bothers him. But
it is this state of perfection that neither Martha nor any other
human being can ever attain. His living for and through Martha,
despite his basic gentleness and goodness, is a form of escape, a
way of dodging a confrontation with his inner self. His fits of
temper and wild assigning of blame to others are further indica-
tions of his self-doubt.

Miss McCarthy has explained that "all the characters in
different ways represent doubt, whether it is philosophical or
ontological" (as in the case of Warren Coe, who questions everything) or self-doubt (as in the case of Martha, who doubts "what
she perceives").[8] Even Miles Murphy, Martha's former husband,
who lives with his new wife and infant son in a neighboring
town and who appears to doubt neither himself nor the constructs of his imagination, doubts the possibility of idealism in
human motivation. Part of Martha's return to New Leeds is involved with a largely unconscious desire to triumph over
the past by proving herself to Miles and thereby eliminating
his spiritual but nonetheless real tyrannical hold on her. As his
wife, she had felt extremely inadequate. Her marriage to John
had restored only some of the confidence that Miles had taken
away. But, by coming back, she and John face the scandal that
had surrounded her separation from Miles seven years before.

Miles Murphy is twenty-five years Martha's senior, "a fat,
freckled fellow with a big frame, a reddish crest of curly hair,
and small, pale-green eyes, like grapes about to burst" (34). The
product of Jesuit schooling, he had studied at Heidelberg, the
Sorbonne, the London School of Economics, and with Jung at
Zurich. His career had been many-faceted and relatively successful, for he had been a playwright, a writer of adventure stories,

a psychologist, a lay analyst, a boxer, a magazine editor, and a practicing mystic.

Martha had met Miles when she had just graduated from college and was acting in a summer theater. At the time, she was engaged to a young architectural student and had "just had a rather squalid abortion, which another young man had paid for. . . ." Then, one evening, she was introduced to Miles who "started bulldozing her into marriage before she really knew him. It was what she needed, he assured her, appraising her with his jellied green eyes when she woke up, for the second time, in bed with him, after a lot of drinks" (103).

Eventually, after four tempestuous years of marriage, she had left him. "Their penultimate quarrel . . . had exploded in the middle of the night, after a party, when she was carrying out two overflowing pails of garbage and he refused, with a sardonic bow, to hold open the screen door for her" (105). Setting down one pail of garbage, she had slapped him across his grinning face with her free hand and had run off into the night to John, who had been vacationing in New Leeds. During the seven years that had elapsed, local gossip had magnified the incident so that Martha had emerged a scarlet woman, although in truth she had not "made love with John until that night or uttered a word against her husband during the twelve afternoons they had talked together on the beach; she had been guilty before, but not with John" (19).

The difficulties arising from resettling in New Leeds are compounded still further by the curious deadlock into which her marriage to John had drifted. Although she and John still love each other, they have fewer illusions about themselves and less hope. They had once agreed that seven years is "the fatal span for love." Yet neither would have chosen to marry anyone else: "From their point of view, for their purposes, they had had the best there was. There lay the bleakness; for them, as they were constituted, through all eternity, this had been the optimum —there was no beyond. There was nothing" (22). Her failure to have a child also disturbs Martha, and she considers their perverse return to New Leeds a "sign" that she is to become pregnant.

And so they settle in their pale-yellow eighteenth-century cottage which they bought because "they were afraid of being afraid to buy it." Reasonably confident that their dislike of the social aspect of the community will act as protection, they attempt to live moderately and creatively. But rational theory and good intentions are impotent against the actualities of existence, as Mary McCarthy's earlier fiction—most notably *The Oasis*—has dramatized. Miles Murphy and Martha have to confront each other; and the "plot" consists in the working out of this inevitability. Fate has two efficient assistants in Warren and Jane Coe, the most popular couple in New Leeds. On the surface, the Coes appear sufficient unto themselves and contented with being "innocent spectators" at the various scandalous performances staged by the other villagers. In actuality, the antics of the New Leedsians provide them with a never-ending and much-needed source of delight and sustenance. Jane, a "big, tawny, ruminative girl" of thirty-eight, is very different from her husband who is as conscientious as she is indolent. Twelve years older than Jane, Warren, who is slightly built and boyishly expectant, "was a very excitable, forward-gazing person, very moralistic and high-principled; every moment was an adventure to him" (31-32). Despite their contrary natures, the Coes share an omnivorous appetite for life: "This greed for experience was their innocent vice."

Before settling in New Leeds, Warren had taught at a school of design, but his stay in this "artistic" community with its population of intellectuals and quasi-intellectuals had introduced him to the infintely more challenging realm of the intellect and to an awareness of the interplay between "knowledge" and art. And his particular mentor is none other than Miles Murphy. Thus the Coes are the agents responsible for the initial inevitable but "unplanned" meeting between Miles and Martha when they invite the Murphys for what has become an annual October picnic on the beach. Later that afternoon, they move indoors to Warren's studio to view a painting of Martha. The portrait, Warren explains, represents the equation upon which the atom bomb is based. In it, he had been experimenting with "something new, a dispersed, explosive cubism, in dark, smoky colors, in which the sitter's personality-nucleus was blown apart into its component solids. There was a geyser of smoke in the middle representing the moment of fission . . ." (53). He envisions his next series as encompassing the principle of the hydrogen bomb or fusion.

Unexpectedly, Miles offers to buy the painting. This decision sets off a discussion of ethics interrupted, of course, by the arrival of Martha and John Sinnott and Dolly Lamb. But nothing catastrophic occurs, and the meeting between Miles and Martha goes peacefully enough. Only Martha knows that she still fears Miles. Her disquiet is heightened by John's failure to recognize her inner agitation: "She had always been able to deceive Miles because he did not know her." Because he refused to consider idealism as a serious factor in life and judged by actions, he "had mistaken both her faults and her virtues." Unlike Miles, John listened to people and paid attention. Martha prized this faculty in her second husband and "wished nothing to be hidden from him, not even the bad parts of her nature. She respected his privacy, because he was a man, but for herself, if she could not be transparent, she did not want to love" (108).

By being able to deceive John about her true feelings, she believes that she has reverted to a former self when, as Miles's wife, she had been forced to practice deception. And she interprets John's failure to perceive her fear as a sign that he, too, does not really know her. Yet, she acknowledges, a part of her nature always has remained hidden even to herself. When she had first met Miles, an "irrational element" had entered her life, and from that time until the present she had failed to understand totally her feelings and actions. She confides these doubts to Dolly Lamb, the only other major character in the novel.

Unmarried and used to being prescribed for, Dolly had taken a cottage in New Leeds in order to paint the marshes because John and Martha had recommended that she do so. Although she shares Martha's self-doubt, her fear has another dimension that her manneristic and decadent paintings reveal. "Every moment of her life was shot through with terrors. . . ." The rustling of trees in the wind or the noise of the icebox running frightened her, and she tried to show in her paintings "the absurd powers that were bending her to their will—nature as animate and threatening and people as elemental forces" (128). Her fear of the inanimate had made her retreat from direct experience, but since her thirtieth birthday the demand to see for herself had become increasingly strong. Unfortunately, New

[128]

Leeds provides her with the wrong kind of person with whom to experience life. The story of her relationship with Sandy Gray, while not advancing the main plot, illustrates admirably the debilitating effects of living in New Leeds and adds to the general air of catastrophe that surrounds the community.

A second and final confrontation between Miles and Martha takes an innocuous enough shape. Again the Coes, as the hosts of a party during which *Bérénice* by Racine is to be read, are responsible. To emphasize the heavy role played by chance in human affairs, Miss McCarthy has Jane Coe receive a telegram announcing the death of Warren's mother. Had she chosen to tell her husband of the news that day, the play-reading would have been cancelled. By arranging to conceal the telegram until the following morning, she "wills" the play-reading and the particular circumstances under which Miles and Martha meet again. In order to clear the stage of as many "extras" as possible, Miles (Helen is home caring for their sick child) and Martha (John is in Boston) arrive at the Coes alone. Not only does Martha attend the play-reading against her better judgment, but she yields to Jane Coe's persuasiveness and agrees to come to the dinner beforehand. This arrangement not only brings her into closer contact with Miles but allows her to consume a good many before-dinner drinks.

In many respects, the play-reading scene is similar to the poetry conference in *The Groves of Academe* or the meetings of the colonists in *The Oasis*. Aside from the ironic parallel between Bérénice and Martha, as the different characters talk, interrupting each other with their questions and points of view, they become known by their ideas. But the insertion of this kind of scene in the middle of a novel of manners is a curious display of literary derring-do. The discussion—which includes snatches of French and Latin and covers such topics as the differences between Racine and Corneille, the function of the unities in classical drama, Plato and the concept of love, doubt and the modern problem play, *Hamlet*, and so on—is interesting and even probable under the circumstances, but it also smacks of the smart bookishness of *Partisan Review*.

But the next scene picks up pace. When John telephones to say that he will not be arriving from Boston for another three or four hours, Martha lingers on at the party with the result that

Miles takes her home. The flesh quickly triumphs over the spirit; for, "an hour and a half later, he was making love to her on the Empire sofa in her parlor. She would not let him carry her into the bedroom, where they could have done their business in comfort. Straining at a gnat and swallowing a camel, as the Good Book said—that was milady Martha" (197). The seduction is seen through Miles's eyes; the immediate aftermath, through Martha's. And the event is undeniably comic.

At first, Miles had been uncertain whether he wanted to dally with Martha or not. But then "the old Adam in him sat up and took notice. They were alone, hubby was gone—why not? . . . He tossed off his highball, wiped his lips, took a quick look at his watch, and started across the room for her" (199). Martha puts up a reasonably good fight, but Miles is persistent. " 'Please don't,' she begged, with tears in her eyes, while he squeezed her nipples between his fingertips; they were hard before he touched them . . ." (201). Finally, however, she takes "a deep breath, like a doomed person," and gives in. But her ardor cools during the time they are undressing and her responses are only half-hearted. Miles detects that she is "trying to hurry him, which made him stubborn, though he was colder than a witch's tit and anxious to get home" (202). Then the realization that she is more than a little drunk makes him remorseful: "Tenderness inflamed his member. Clasping her fragile body brusquely to him, he thrust himself into her with short, quick strokes. A gasp of pain came from her, and it was over" (202-3).

With Miles on his way back to Digby and Helen, Miss Mc-Carthy switches again to the vocal consciousness of Martha who is busily picking up the beads that had spilled when her necklace had broken in the amorous play of the hour before. "Miles had not enjoyed it much either, Martha said pensively to herself. . . ." She knows that she should never have invited him to have a nightcap. "But it had been one of those challenges that she always rose to, like a fish to the bait—the fear of being afraid" (204). Rather drunkenly, she rationalizes her folly and goes to bed.

The next advance in the plot is in the way of a discovery. Martha finds out that she is pregnant. Instead of being joyous, she is deeply unhappy because of the very slight possibility that Miles might be the father of the child. Because her natural inclination is to have the baby and say nothing to John, she decides to have an abortion. "The hardest course was the right one. . . . If her nature shrank from the task, if it hid and cried piteously for mercy, that was a sign that she was in the presence of the ethical" (262). On the credit side, her sleeping with Miles that night had served to free her from the past, and she knows that "he held no further interest or terror for her. He was as dead as a clinker."

She solves the problem of getting money for the abortion by enlisting the sympathies of Warren Coe, and, in a spurt of energy, she finishes the play, thereby fulfilling the second reason for coming back to New Leeds. "It was like a fairy tale, in which you got your wish, but in such a way that you wished you had not wished it" (275). But Martha's preoccupation and restlessness are apparent to John, who interprets her strange behavior as a sign that she no longer loves him. Finally out of patience when she goes off to the Coes alone for tea (they were to have dinner elsewhere and one of their "rules" was never to accept more than one invitation per day), he decides to leave her. Then, realizing suddenly that it was December, he has "the clue to Martha's strange behavior. . . . She was thinking about Christmas. . . . She set foolish feminine store by anniversaries and holidays and loved to prepare surprises" (307). Sadness and love at her eternal childishness replace his anger, and he discards the notion of leaving her.

Martha, in the meantime, had eagerly rushed to the Coes to receive the money that Warren had secured for her at considerable sacrifice and with great secrecy. Driving back from the Coes, who had urged her to stay for cocktails with the local poetess, Eleanor Considine, she feels exultantly happy and anxious to return to John. "Eleanor Considine, a woman of fifty, with dyed red hair and a long amatory history, was a cautionary example of everything Martha was trying not to be" (310). Martha had avoided meeting her because she wanted to be above the pettiness of the older woman's jealousy. Warren's stoutheartedness and cleverness in getting the money had made her feel as though she were in the presence of the sublime. And she is certain that whether eventually she tells John or not, everything will be all right between them.

Confident in a way that she had not been since she had met

Miles, she knows that she is "no longer afraid of herself. That was the reward of that fearsome decision, which no longer seemed fearsome, now that it was behind her." She laughs and steps on the gas and, thinking of Warren, sings, " '*Integer vitae, scelerisque purus*' " [a man upright in life and free from guilt]. Then, around a blind curve, she sees the headlights of an oncoming automobile. Reason tells her that the rapidly approaching car is that of Eleanor Considine en route to the Coes. "Martha slowed down and hugged her own side of the road. As the car crashed into her and she heard a shower of glass, she knew, in a wild flash of humor, that she had made a fatal mistake: in New Leeds, after sundown, she would have been safer on the wrong side of the road." (312-13).

The ironic ending *is* implicit in the first chapter, and the middle section is heavy with the theme of "death in life." Without question, the ending has thematic inevitability. Unlike Mulcahy whose instinct for self-preservation allows him not only to endure but to triumph within the academy, Martha, Miss McCarthy has explained, by admitting to herself that she is pregnant and recognizing that she must do something about it, "becomes mortal."[9] But the decision to have an abortion, by affording her mortality, results in her exclusion from the charmed circle and the company of "all those drunks and human odds and ends" with their miraculous powers of survival. Accordingly, "she gets killed—to get killed is simply a symbol of the fact that she's mortal."[10]

Martha Sinnott has moved, therefore, from the category of the comic character with his guarantee of immortality to that of the heroine who exists in time and is capable of growth. What is ironic—or possibly simply weak—is that Martha achieves mortality or humanity through deciding to kill life. As Louis Auchincloss has observed, her passionate concern for the truth and her own moral position rule out the possibility of her giving "birth to a child of whose paternity she can never be sure."[11] But a decision of this sort is seldom considered to be a manifestation of any particular inner strength. Also, since her first abortion is treated summarily, the significance of the decision to undergo a second loses force. But Martha's willingness to have this particular abortion as a result of the circumstances surrounding her pregnancy represents her triumph over Miles and self-doubt or, collectively, the past. Paradoxically, her new-found courage makes her ill-equipped to lead the uncharming charmed life of the New Leedsians and so she dies.

Esthetically, however, this ending is unsuccessful. The contrivance is too obvious. By making Eleanor Considine the instrument of death, Mary McCarthy resorts to a *dea ex machina*. In "The Fact in Fiction," she declared, "There are no gods in the novel and no machinery for them; to speak, even metaphorically, of a *deus ex machina* in a novel—that is, of the entrance of a providential figure from above—is to imply a shortcoming. . . ."[12] The alcoholic poetess is a completely providential figure, for she does not exist until the last few pages—at least she receives no mention until then. Miss McCarthy has to interrupt Martha's happy reveries as she is driving back from the Coes to give a thumb-nail sketch of Eleanor Considine and her "long amatory history." Very neatly, Miss McCarthy has her represent the kind of person that Martha would most like *not* to be. Yet, in the weird world of *A Charmed Life*, there is an ironic appropriateness in Martha's getting killed by a person peripheral to her own existence and by one whom she mildly scorns. So the fairy-tale element in *A Charmed Life* can be made to excuse the sudden appearance of Eleanor Considine, but this same highly artificial contrivance can be used against classifying this work as a novel according to Miss McCarthy's own definition. In *The Paris Review* interview, she has acknowledged that perhaps none of her books can be properly considered novels.

II *Some Critical Reactions to* A Charmed Life

Josephine Herbst notes that the contrived coincidence of the ending, by allowing Martha "to bypass genuine experience," leaves the reader and the protagonist nowhere.[13] This criticism, of course, points out the problem central to that of narrative mimicry. The intention of the novelist is not made clear. What does Martha's death mean? Miss McCarthy has described Martha's dying as inevitable because it represents her moving from immortality to mortality. But where is the larger lesson? The implication is too narrow. To make the meaning of Martha's death have wider application, one would have to posit that learning to triumph over the past and self-doubt is a sign of mortality and leads to an immediate death—obviously a ridiculous assumption. Or, following a slightly different line of reasoning, one would have to say that in New Leeds this kind of fearlessness results in death—a somewhat more acceptable supposition. But New Leeds does not represent a microcosm of any larger reality. What "meaning" and "satire" *A Charmed Life* possesses are part of a closed and finite circuit and have relevance primarily in terms of the fictional world that Mary McCarthy describes.

Reviewers have noted that segments of *A Charmed Life* are autobiographical. New Leeds is identified usually as Wellfleet, Massachusetts, and Miles Murphy as based on Edmund Wilson. Such assigning of "real life" identities, of course, adds nothing to the novel which, being far larger than autobiography, is a clever distortion of life. And, as Mary McCarthy has said, Miles Murphy cannot possibly be Edmund Wilson because Miles is tall and writes successful plays, and Wilson is short and " 'everybody knows that Edmund never had a successful play in his life!' "[14] Her dismissal neglects with a tongue-in-cheek nicety the similarities that do exist between Wilson and Miles Murphy.

And there are other parallels. The "real" Mary McCarthy shares the fictional John and Martha Sinnott's belief that seven years is "the fatal span for love." In a moment of marital despair, Miss McCarthy once told her brother Kevin "that no two people should be *allowed* to stay married for more than seven years, unless they could prove in court that they *should*."[15] Also, Martha leaves Miles Murphy under conditions similar to those of Miss McCarthy's own abrupt departure from Wilson. But all that is past history. What is interesting is simply that, as Miss McCarthy matures as a writer, she continues to draw heavily from her own experience. In *The Group*, she keeps up this sometimes questionable practice and carries her ventriloquial act to, and perhaps beyond, its esthetic limitations.

III *The Machinations of Vassar-ness*

Mary McCarthy has a penchant for describing a collection of persons defined by some social condition. *The Group* (1963), with its eight insiders and one outsider, simply extends the pattern started in *The Company She Keeps* and continued in *The Oasis, The Groves of Academe,* and *A Charmed Life.* In all these works, the necessity of paying attention to a number of different characters causes a lack of focus. And, in addition, the long arm of coincidence is usually too noticeable, especially in *The Group* because of its nine heroines and because the novel begins after the girls have graduated from Vassar College. Such an arrangement allows them to roam more or less freely and prevents their being cooped up within the Vassar gates or confined to a mountaintop or to the campus of an experimental college or to an artists' colony on Cape Cod. New York City provides what sense of community *The Group* contains.

Like these other works, *The Group* is satirical, "a kind of mock-chronicle novel. . . . about the idea of progress . . . . seen in the female sphere, the feminine sphere. You know, home economics, architecture, domestic technology, contraception, child-bearing; the study of technology in the home, in the play-pen, in the bed. It's supposed to be the history of the loss of faith in progress, in the idea of progress, during that twenty year period."[16] But *The Group* does not cover a span of twenty years. The novel begins in June, 1933, and ends in July, 1940. Sometime during 1961 or 1962, Miss McCarthy abandoned her plan of stopping the novel with the inauguration of Eisenhower in 1953 and settled on the present scheme of encompassing only seven years.

Her own esthetic theories are responsible for her giving up her initial plan. As she explained to the *Paris Review* interviewer, "These girls are all essentially comic figures, and it's awfully hard to make anything happen to them."[17] Yet, to achieve any verisimilitude at all, she would have to depict *some* development or growth in her characters during the course of twenty years; and, following the argument she outlines in "Characters in Fiction," comic characters cannot develop: "the capacity to learn, from experience or instruction, is what is forbidden to all comic creations and to what is comic in you and me."[18] This problem caused Miss McCarthy to abandon *The Group*—which she had begun "around the time of the Stevenson campaign" or shortly after completing *The Groves of Academe*—to write *A Charmed Life* (1955), *Venice Observed* (1956), *Memories of a Catholic Girlhood* (1957), and *The Stones of Florence* (1959); she did not return to the novel until early in 1960.[19]

Quite understandably, she seized upon a device for *The Group* that she had used with considerable thematic success in *A*

Charmed Life, an "occurrence" that allows her to deal with time. She has one of the girls develop or become mortal and, like Martha Sinnott, die as a result. In *The Group,* Kay Strong Petersen, the "most" central character in the novel, develops. At least, this is a possible interpretation. Kay moves out of the category of a comic character by falling (accidentally or purposefully—no one is certain) from the window of her room on the twentieth floor of the Vassar Club in New York City. And what was she doing at the time? Why, leaning out the window spotting airplanes. As one of the characters says, " 'You might say . . . that Kay was the first American war casualty.' "[20] Such conjecturing is both neat and ironic. After all, Vassar *is* responsible for Kay's development or "birth" by having offered her a chance to become educated. And what Vassar giveth, Vassar hath the right to take away. Or is Vassar College to blame? Perhaps men (represented by Harald Petersen) are responsible. Or maybe the whole drift of society and the false god of progress are at fault. But the blame cannot be assigned because Miss McCarthy has submerged her voice into that of her nine heroines and three of their mothers.

This twelve-faceted ventriloquial act accounts for the tonal shifts that take place within and between chapters. The best sections occur when Miss McCarthy gets all the girls babbling at once and then breaks in to show the reader what certain of the characters are thinking privately. The weakest chapters are those in which she is mimicking someone like Libby MacAusland or Priss Hartshorn. Miss McCarthy succeeds in reproducing the educated banality of their speech, but the effect is tedious. In "Characters in Fiction," she points out that often a reader complains that an author's style is full of clichés "when that, precisely, is the point."[21] But the reader has the right to complain if the impersonation is overdone. Libby MacAusland *is* "a duncey broad," and the sections on "Duncy" (as Norman Mailer persists rightfully in calling her) are annoying.[22]

The Group, with its collective protagonist, is obviously not totally autobiographical. But bits and pieces of Mary McCarthy and her life have found their way into this novel too. Like the "group," Miss McCarthy graduated from Vassar College in June, 1933; and, like Kay Strong, she married a week after graduation. Her first husband, Harold Johnsrud, bore some resemblance to the fictional Harald Petersen. Johnsrud, like the Harald of *The Group,* was the son of a school administrator who had been a scapegoat in an academic scandal. As an adult, Johnsrud had "brooded over his father's misfortune . . . and this had given his nature a sardonic twist that inclined him to behave like a paradox—to follow the mode and despise it, . . . play bridge with society couples and poker with the stage electricians, dress in the English style and carry a walking stick while wearing a red necktie."[23] And, like Harald Petersen, he wrote plays—unsuccessfully. Also, Mary McCarthy and Johnsrud had taken part in "a consumers' walkout at the Waldorf to support a waiters' strike" as do the fictional Kay and Harald Petersen and Norine and Put Blake.[24]

"The Vassar Girl" describes Miss McCarthy's own undergraduate identification with the "aesthetes" (followers of Miss Sandison and traditional scholarship) as opposed to the Socialists (protegées of Miss Lockwood and an emphasis on sociology). The rift between the two factions is important in *The Group,* for it sets Norine (a Miss Lockwood girl) apart from the eight members of the group. Also, in the novel, Miss McCarthy has Harald Petersen see a Vassar College production (*The Winter's Tale*) that Kay directed. In real life, Johnsrud witnessed *The Winter's Tale* in which Miss McCarthy, during her senior year, played the part of Leontes. Additionally, Miss McCarthy's experiences as a book reviewer in the 1930's provided, in all probability, much of the information she used in the section about Libby MacAusland and her career.

Vassar College gave her also the "real life" models for the girls in *The Group.* Miss McCarthy acknowledges that "some of them are drawn pretty much from life, and some of them are rather composite. I've tried to keep myself out of this book. Oh, and all their mothers are in it. That's the part I almost like the best."[25] But Dottie, she explains, referring to Chapter III (printed first as "Dottie Makes An Honest Woman of Herself" in *Partisan Review* [January-February, 1954]), " 'isn't like that at all. That never happened to her. The incident is entirely fictional. I saw Dottie recently, and she hasn't changed a bit.' "[26] Once again Miss McCarthy is "inventing" but with her eye on the object.

Although Mary McCarthy began *The Group* without knowing how and where she was going to end it, the first chapter foreshadows the conclusion in much the same manner as the first chapter of *The Groves of Academe* or *A Charmed Life*. Mulcahy knows that he is going to get reinstated and plots his initial strategy accordingly. Martha and John Sinnott know that they should have avoided returning to New Leeds and are fearful of the consequences of their act. Miss McCarthy is good at beginnings and at paradoxes. But the endings, resting as they do on paradoxes, fail to resolve the problem of intention. And, of course, the device of narrative mimicry excludes the possibility of the author's supplying an intention. The conclusion of *The Group* is ambiguous also, for Miss McCarthy has simply presented another paradox in the supposed triumph of Elinor Eastlake.

Chapter One, however, gets *The Group* off to a good start by introducing the major characters, establishing the theme of progress, and hinting at impending disaster. The first sentence reads: "It was June, 1933, one week after Commencement, when Kay Leiland Strong, Vassar '33, the first of her class to run around the table at the Class Day dinner, was married to Harald Petersen, Reed '27, in the chapel of St. George's Church, P. E., Karl F. Reiland, Rector." Names, place, dates . . . and then the odd bit of information that Kay, in the language of one of the many Vassar traditions, had been the first of her class to announce her engagement. In this chapter, Miss McCarthy mimics not only individual voices but the collective voice of the group. This collective mimicry provides a "voice" or style well suited to the purposes of the mock-chronicle: "They were in the throes of discovering New York, imagine it, when some of them had actually lived here all their lives, in tiresome Georgian houses full of waste space in the Eighties or Park Avenue apartment buildings . . ." (3).

To the group, the unorthodoxy of Kay's wedding is both thrilling and frightening. At first, as they take their places in the almost empty chapel, they marvel at the absence of "any older person." Kay's having "lived with" Harald strikes them as defiant, and they accept as rightly unconventional the newlyweds' returning later that day to the unmade bed (if they knew Kay) in the apartment that she and Harald were subletting for the summer. Harald's having to be at the theater that evening had precluded the possibility of a honeymoon: "This seemed to them very exciting and of course it justified the oddities of the wedding. Kay and Harald were too busy and dynamic to let convention cramp their style" (4). The Depression had introduced a new code of behavior fashioned on a new reality. "Even among their own number, one girl had had to accept a scholarship to finish college, and nobody thought the worse of her for it: Polly Andrews remained one of their *very* dearest friends. They were a different breed, they could assure the curate, from the languid buds of the previous decade: there was not one of them who did not propose to work this coming fall. . . ." Each shares the belief that "the worst fate" would lie in becoming "stuffy and frightened" like Mother and Dad. And each has vowed not to marry a banker or broker or corporation lawyer. "They would rather be wildly poor and live on salmon wiggle than be forced to marry one of those dull purplish young men of their own set . . ." (11).

Yet the dignity and solemnity of the ceremony itself disturbs them. All at once, the absence of parents or older persons seems "queer and ominous," and Kay and Harald's premarital relationship fills them with a "sudden sense of the unsanctioned" (9). Even the religiosity of the rector's words assumes a disquieting significance in the light of Kay's self-announced scientific atheism. But the wedding breakfast, given by the bride and groom, renews their courage somewhat. As a group, they are impressed favorably by Harald's obvious dedication to the theater and his knowledge of food and alcohol. "They were very much interested, just at this time, in receipts for drinks; they all adored brandy Alexanders and White Ladies and wanted to hear about a cocktail called the Clover Club that was one-third gin, one-third lemon juice, one-third grenadine, and the white of an egg" (18). Cooking interests them also, for they had grown tired of unimaginative chops and roasts and were anxious "to try new combinations and foreign recipes and puffy omelets and soufflés and interesting aspics and just one hot dish in a Pyrex, no soup, and a fresh green salad" (25).

The group is in high spirits (despite Kay's having worn a touch of black and having invited thirteen guests to the breakfast) when they see the newlyweds off for their honeymoon at Coney Island. At the station platform, one of Harald's guests sings "My girl's from Vassar; none can surpass'er." Undaunted by the stares of passers-by, Kay tosses her bouquet over the turnstile to the waiting girls who, showering the nuptial pair with rice provided unexpectedly by Lakey, agree later that, "banal or not," the rice had been "just the little touch that had been needed to round off an unforgettable occasion" (29).

As well as providing a collective portrait of the group, the first chapter focuses briefly on each of the girls. Most important, of course, is Kay Strong Petersen, who, in this chapter, is seen only through the eyes of the other members of the group. Mingled with their fondness and admiration for Kay is a mild mistrust. When they had first met her, she had been a "shy, pretty, somewhat heavy Western girl with black lustrous curly hair and a wild-rose complexion, active in hockey, in the choir, given to large tight brassières and copious menstruations. . . ." Vassar had changed her into a "thin, hard-driving, authoritative young woman, dressed in dungarees, sweat shirt, and sneakers, with smears of paint in her unwashed hair, tobacco stains on her fingers," who addressed her friends by their last names, and counseled "premarital experiment and the scientific choice of a mate. Love, she said, was an illusion." But the group considers Kay's bark to be worse than her bite and believes her early marriage proof of this assumption. Still, her tendency to aggrandize her situation and her being oblivious to social nuances make them aware that she is "a little bit of an outsider," a fact not really conditional upon her coming from Salt Lake City.

Elinor Eastlake, Kay's "discoverer," had considered her to be "malleable" and "capable of learning." But, after bringing Kay into the group, her interest in her "discovery" had waned. In her estimation, "there was a spiritual obstacle to the marriage; she considered Kay a *cruel, ruthless, stupid* person who was marrying Harald from ambition" (9). This harshness on Lakey's part and her inscrutability fascinate the other girls and make them suspect great profundity. "The girls she chose to collect were mystified, usually, by what she saw in them; they humbly perceived that they were very different from her" (16). Yet it is Lakey who slips away after the ceremony to buy rice, the traditional symbol of fertility and happiness.

The other members of the group do not share Lakey's intense mortification at the wrongness of the wedding although Pokey (Mary) Prothero, "a fat cheerful New York society girl with big red cheeks and yellow hair, who talked like a jolly beau of the

McKinley period, in imitation of her yachtsman father," notices Kay's black heels and hat. Like Elinor Eastlake, who is going to Europe to study art history, Pokey is beginning graduate studies. Her plan is to attend Cornell Agricultural School and take up veterinary science. Without subtleties and unencumbered by middle-class morality and concern over the petty details of existence, she accepts good-naturedly the burden of privilege, peering at the world through weak sapphire eyes and a *lorgnon* of diamonds, and commenting on people and places in a "grating society caw." The possible invalidity of the marriage upsets Dorothy Renfrew, a basically conventional, rich girl from Boston and a devout Episcopal communicant. Dottie, constitutionally rather delicate, was often teased by the others "for her decorum and staid habits and mufflers and medicines and the long mink coat she wore on campus to keep off the cold, but she had a good sense of humor and quietly joined in the laugh." Brown-eyed, with a rather long nose ("in the pointed New England way") and black, heavy brows, she "resembled the Copley portrait of an ancestress that hung in the family hall" (23). But Dottie, as she suspects and as the reader finds, is fun-loving and moderately sensuous.

The remaining members of the group accept more or less un-hesitatingly the peculiarities of the wedding. For Libby Mac-Ausland, the interest in Kay's marriage lies, apparently, in its gossip value. ". . . A tall, pretty blonde with perpetually dilating brown eyes, a long, arching, inquisitive neck, and a manner of anxious conviviality," she had been sophomore class president and "had just missed being elected president of Students" (15). Helena Davison, Kay's bridesmaid, is seen in the first chapter only through the collective consciousness of the group. All that is learned about her at this time is that she comes from Cleveland where her family lives on the income of their income and that she had roomed with Kay during their junior year. Polly Andrews, too, is mentioned only briefly. Her after-graduation plans are "to work as a technician in the new Medical Center." The last member of the group is Priss Hartshorn, "a solemn, ashy-haired little girl who looked like a gopher. . . ." The previous day, Priss "had simultaneously announced her engagement to a young doctor and landed a job with the N.R.A." (11).

These are the eight members of the group. Yet a substantial portion of the plot revolves around the activities and ideas of Norine Schmittlapp who, although Vassar '33, stands outside the group and is not present at the wedding. As an undergraduate, Norine had been a political (one of Miss Lockwood's girls). What separates her from the others is a particular kind of un- feelingness and an apparent unawareness of any tradition at all. Although she envies the members of the group, she despises them for their lack of emotionality. But she does get involved with the group (in particular Kay) after graduation and, by contrast, emphasizes their "groupiness."

Mary McCarthy has long been accused of not creating very likeable male characters. And the men in her short stories and novels, if they are treated in any depth, are either mildly re- pellent Babbitts such as Jim Barnett, the Yale man, or grandly unattractive egoists such as Henry Mulcahy or Miles Murphy. Often, however, the male character is treated summarily through the consciousness of the heroine (as in "The Weeds"). This kind of summary characterization is especially true in *The Group*. But with eight or nine heroines, Miss McCarthy does not have time to develop the male characters. The single exception is Harald Petersen who, unquestionably, is nearly as obnoxious as Miles Murphy and as detestable as Henry Mulcahy. However, putting the shoe on the other foot, the Vassar girls are not particularly virtuous or attractive either. Lakey is the only beauty of the group. The sterile intelligence of Helena lacks direction. None possesses any distinctive talent. Neither extremely good nor ex- tremely bad, they represent—in a somewhat exaggerated fashion —their class and kind.

But, without doubt, the male characters are considerably less appealing, singularly and collectively, than the group. And none of the girls is so overtly destructive and malicious as Harald Petersen. Harald is obviously the "wrong" husband for Kay, yet his contemporaneousness makes him an obvious choice. Early in their marriage, Kay finds a letter that he has written and never mailed to his father. In this letter, he admits his fear of life and his respect for Kay's courage and "pioneer confidence." Kay, he reasons, is fearless because she is ignorant of life's cruelty. The letter continues, " 'Don't ask whether I love her; love, apart from chemical attraction, is still an unknown quantity to me. . . . She's a very strong young woman with a radiant, still-undisciplined vitality'" (82-83). But Harald's inner uncertainty makes him incapable of giving Kay's energies shape and form (as he professes a desire to do), and he succeeds only in destroying her spirit. On the other hand, by being afraid to see the "real" Harald and by setting levels of attainment impossible for him to reach, Kay is the partial agent of her own destruction.

The other husbands have their problems too. Putnam Blake, Norine Schmittlapp's first husband, is co-founder of an independent fund-raising organization for labor and left-wing causes, "a thin, white-faced young man with a close collegiate haircut, an unsmiling expression, and a low, tense voice . . ." (98). The only trouble with Put is that he is impotent, a circumstance responsible for Norine's falling into the arms of Harald. Her second husband, Freddy Rogers (his family had changed their name from Rosenberg when they had converted to Episcopalianism) is acceptable; but he is a banker. Although a product of Choate and Princeton, he is Norine's intellectual inferior, or so she believes. "'Our Vassar education made it tough for me to accept my womanly role. While Freddy, as a Jew, instinctively adopts the matriarchal principle. . . . Freddy's philoprogenitive. . . . So long as I can breed, I'm a sacred cow to him. Bed's very important to Freddy; he's a sensualist, like Solomon. Collects erotica. He worships me because I'm a goy'" (344).

Priss Hartshorn's husband, Sloan Crockett, is a budding pediatrician and a staunch Republican, "a tall young man with glasses and an Arrow-collar profile who had worked his way through medical school" (227). Sloan's only drawback is a lack of sensitivity that permits him to use his wife and infant son as guinea pigs to test his medical theories. Only Polly Andrews' husband, Jim Ridgeley, seems really admirable. Although a bit impulsive, he is competent, protective, and intelligent.

The boy friends are no better than the husbands. Gus LeRoy, who had been Polly's lover for nearly a year prior to her engagement to Jim, is a weak, self-pitying man. A Communist sympathizer and a moderately successful editor, he seemed to Polly the most normal man she had met. "He watched his waistline and checked up on young Gus's visits to the pediatrician, who was one of the best younger men in the city, like Gus's analyst, who had been Brill's favorite pupil" (251). Eventually, however, Gus returns to his wife and their young son. At that time, Polly realizes that he is ordinary: "That was what was the matter with him."

Only a brief view is given of Libby MacAusland's would-be seducer, Nils Aslund, "a genuine Norwegian baron" and a ski jumper. "He had the most heavenly manners and a marvelous figure and danced divinely" (209-10). But his manners desert him when he tries to seduce Libby after her party. Her struggles to protect her quaint honor amuse him until he discovers that she is a virgin. Disgusted, he calls her a bore and leaves her in a state of undress and dismay. Last in what Norman Mailer describes as "the endless gallery of Mary McCarthy's feverish, loud-talking, drunken, neurotic, crippled, and jargon-compensated louts" is Dick Brown, one of Harald's wedding guests.[27] "He looked very much the artist—handsome as a piece of Roman statuary but somewhat battered and worn; the muscles of the cheeks were loosening, and there were somber creases on either side of the flawless, straight, strong nose" (19). A commercial artist, and without much money, Dick is an ex-expatriate, living in a furnished room in Greenwich Village. His meeting with Dottie at the wedding breakfast leads quickly to their brief affair.

Chapters two through fourteen provide a substantial and satirical chronicle of innovations in the feminine sphere. The sections on Dottie Renfrew (Chapters two and three) illustrate the "new" attitude toward sex and the "new" technology of contraception. The clinically objective description of Dottie's first night of love-making is humorous because of its factuality and in its comical attention to details is similar to some of the sexual encounters in the novels of Henry Miller. Although a little drunk, Dick is an efficient, capable, and considerate lover. And Dottie, despite her Vassar education and Dick's warning that he does not love her, enjoys her seduction. In the passages concerning Dottie's visit to a birth-control bureau and her appointment for a "fitting," Mary McCarthy's penchant for facts runs rampant. Not only does she discuss the diaphragm (origin, description, and method of insertion), but she describes the etiquette of contraception. And here Harald is helpful. Riding with Dottie "on top of a Fifth Avenue bus" to the doctor's office, Kay repeats what Harald has told her about protocol in the matter of contraception, a code of manners which, like any other etiquette, had to be studied in terms of economics. "No man of honor (which Dick, in Harald's opinion, was) would expect a girl to put up the doctor's fee, plus the price of the pessary and the jelly and the douche bag unless he planned to sleep with her long enough for her to recover her investment" (54). The custodianship of the contraceptive equipment, according to Harald, had the nature of a sacred trust that the man assumed—based, of course, on the impracticality of the girl's keeping the diaphragm in her apartment.

The question-and-answer period prior to the pelvic examination and the actual fitting is as comic as Dottie's subsequent struggles to learn how to insert the diaphragm correctly. Eventually, however, she "learns"; and, leaving Kay, she buys a fountain syringe at a nearby drugstore and telephones Dick. Receiving no answer, she walks into Washington Square Park where—amid the sounds of children playing and "some young Jewish men" arguing—she sits on a bench to wait, the paraphernalia reposing awkwardly on her lap. The failure to reach Dick after several more attempts results in her hiding her purchases beneath a bench and walking out of the park alone. "A cruising taxi picked her up at the corner and drove her, quietly sobbing, to the Vassar Club. The next morning early, before the town was stirring, she took the train for Boston" (71).

And back to Mother, who belongs to the Chilton Club. The four mothers who appear in *The Group* serve as an ironic contrast to the "progress" represented by their daughters. The mothers (with one exception, and she does not count because wealth and stupidity have insulated her from the world at large) are more forward-looking and certainly more compassionate than their daughters. Mrs. Renfrew, for example, after finding out some time later about Dottie's affair with Dick Brown, is immediately sympathetic. Almost without hesitation, she advises her daughter to postpone her impending wedding to a wealthy Arizonian widower in order to make certain of her true feelings toward Dick. Dottie, however, refuses adamantly to accept her mother's counsel. "Distractedly, Mrs. Renfrew was aware of the oddity of this situation, in which the roles were reversed, and the daughter was hurrying herself into a 'suitable' marriage while the mother was pleading with her to seek out an unsuitable rake" (177). Dottie, of course, has her way. And that is the last of Dottie, as far as the reader is concerned; she reappears only twice and then in very insignificant roles. Lakey, during this interval, is still in Europe. Pokey Prothero, married and living in New Jersey, is given only brief mention. Helena Davison is present but is not a vital force. The necessity of dealing with eight "heroines" causes this dropping and picking up of characters. Unfortunately, some of the more potentially interesting characters (like Pokey) are arbitrarily dismissed.

Miss McCarthy allows three of the mothers to "reveal" themselves through the unifying device of a sympathy strike during which (according to the *Times* and *Tribune*) Harald Petersen and Putnam Blake were arrested. The newspaper accounts mention that the "strikers" included, among such literary celebrities as Dorothy Parker and Alexander Woollcott, "a number of Vassar girls." Mrs. Renfrew, "a cheerful, lively person who always looked on the gay side of things," accepts the matter casually, imagining that "it must have been quite an adventure for those radical young people to get dressed up and do battle with the hotel staff, rather like a *Lampoon* prank . . ." (165).

The other mothers are not so liberally disposed toward Vassar's participation in the strike as Mrs. Renfrew. Mrs. Prothero, a huge and "delicate" lady, is incapacitated by the scandal. Placing the blame on higher education and on Vassar College for their once having had Harald Petersen for dinner, she directs the butler, Hatton, to burn the newspaper clipping. "'A jailbird!' she repeated indignantly, with a wobble of her receding chin, so loud that Yvonne, coming down the stairs, could hear her. Clutching her wrapper around her and holding Yvonne's arm, she retired upstairs to her bedroom and canceled the car, which was to take her to the hairdresser at eleven" (163-64).

Mrs. Davison takes the affair with better grace and with an attitude of "comfortable and dignified alarm." She tells her daughter, "'I said to your father that what this fracas reminded me of was the old suffragette demonstrations. Chaining themselves to lampposts, and that young woman, Inez Something Something, Vassar she was too, who rode a white horse down Fifth Avenue to demonstrate for the vote. Dressed to kill'" (147). But then Mrs. Davison is a singular individual, and, although she and her husband have a great deal of money, they do not have the social status of the Protheros. Also, unlike Mrs. Prothero, Mrs. Davison is reasonably intelligent and well-read.

A fourth mother, Mrs. Hartshorn, is described in the chapter
that discusses Priss and the issue of breast-feeding. After having
had three miscarriages, Priss gives birth to a boy. To please her
pediatrician husband and to demonstrate his belief in the im-
munizing properties of a mother's milk, she agrees to breast-feed
their child. During her convalescence, her friends gather on week-
end afternoons in her room at New York Hospital for cocktails.
Mrs. Hartshorn, swallowing "her martini in a single draft, like
medicine" in "the style among advanced society women of her
age," mocks good-humoredly Sloan's championing of breast-feeding. As she explains to Polly Andrews, " 'Just fancy little Priss being the first of your set to do it. . . . She's so flat there she's never
had to wear a brassière. But Sloan says it's not the size that counts.
I do hope he's right.' " Doctors, she observes, are all theory:
" 'The bottle was the war cry of my generation. . . . For us, the
bottle spelled the end of colic, and the frantic young husband
walking the baby all night. We swore by the bottle, we of the
avant-garde.' " She also complains that medicine is all cycles:
" 'First we nursed our babies, then science told us not to. Now
it tells us we were right in the first place. Or were we wrong
then but would be right now?' " (227-28). Her question goes
unanswered.

Other members of the group, in their different ways, also
represent "progress." The chapter dealing with Libby MacAusland depicts the Vassar graduate as career girl. The special circumstances and procedures involved in having an affair with a
married man (Gus LeRoy is only separated from his wife) are
illustrated in the sections concerning Polly Andrews. A mild-
mannered description of the Depression and the accompanying
readjustment of certain social attitudes is given in the chapter
depicting the arrival and settling of Polly's father in New York
City. The sections on Kay and her life with Harald illustrate
some of the advanced concepts in the areas of architecture,
furniture, and home economics. Kay admires "the smart new
renovated tenements in the Fifties and Eighties, along the East
River, black with white trim and white Venetian blinds. . . . A
lot of waste space was being eliminated in these buildings—no
more foyers or dining rooms, which were obsolete conventions"
(61-62). House furnishings, too, were to be simple and functional.

America, she and Harald believe, is moving toward a glorious technocracy. Ironically, Kay is the first to be destroyed in the modern world she had propounded so valiantly.

Priss Hartshorn Crockett, through a chance meeting with Norine Schmittlapp Blake Rogers, figures again in Chapter Fourteen. Norine, like Priss, is in the habit of taking her son to Central Park; there the two girls meet and discover that they are neighbors. After gossiping for a while, they settle down to a discussion of the ideology of bringing up children. Priss, following her husband's theories, believes in a well-planned diet and regular mealtimes, a permissive yet firm attitude toward toilet-training, and an avoidance of injurious or unsanitary playthings. As an infant, Stephen had never been picked up when he had cried except to be given a drink of water or to have his diaper changed. And, at two and a-half years old, he went to bed without putting up a fight and was well-behaved and self-sufficient. Priss advocates measurement and the establishing of norms. She asks Norine, "'Have you heard about Gesell's studies at Yale? Finally we're going to have a scientific picture of the child. Gesell shows us what to expect in terms of achievement of a one-year-old, a two-year-old, a three-year-old. When he publishes his findings in p-p-popular form, every mother will have a y-yard-stick'" (342-43). The only evidence of failure in Sloan's system is Stephen's steadfast refusal to be toilet trained—a willfulness, Priss thinks to herself, that is a signal of his private rebellion against his regimented life.

Norine, on the other hand, opposes regimen. Her three-month-old son Ichabod is on demand feeding, goes to bed at random hours, and already chooses some of his food. Norine plans neither to wean nor to toilet train her son because, as she explains, he needs "the fun of playing with his own excrement," just as he needs sucking. Norine bases her views on anthropology. "'I'm burned out on politics. . . . Since Munich. My passion's comparative religion. Society is finished if it can't find its way back to God'" (334). She dismisses Gesell as a "'fossil relic of behaviorism'" and pushes Priss' talk about measurements aside with the observation, "'You still believe in progress. . . . I'd forgotten there were people who did. It's your substitute for religion. Your tribal totem is the yardstick. But we've transcended all that. No first-rate mind can accept the concept of progress any more.'" She claims that true radicalism means "'going back to the roots. The New Deal is rootless—superficial'" (343). Priss, from that day on, avoided the section of the Park where she had met Norine.

Mary McCarthy has described *The Group* as a "history of the loss of faith in progress." Yet she gives to Norine, the outsider, the denunciation of progress that is the implicit moral of the book. Norine, however, cannot be trusted. Her championing of the cultural anthropologists and her advocacy of a neo-orthodoxy is simply another twist in the whole notion of progress, in reality a "retrogression" similar in some respects to Sloan's advocacy of breast feeding. Also, her sweeping generalizations illustrate that her mind is still sophomoric and that she has not learned. But her strange power of endurance does allow her to emerge somewhat victorious in the last chapter. Although she had not been invited to Kay's wedding, she attends Kay's funeral and brings Ichabod, entrenched in a sling, with her.

Kay's funeral permits Mary McCarthy to reassemble all the members of the group except Dottie. The time is July, 1940, and the place, the Episcopal Church on Stuyvesant Square where Kay had been married. "This time the service was being held in the church itself; there were too many mourners to fit in the chapel" (355). Even three of the mothers are present, Mrs. Hartshorn, Mrs. Davison, and Mrs. Renfrew. And Lakey has returned from Europe with her baroness in tow. The ambiguity surrounding Kay's death is useful to Miss McCarthy. After Kay's nervous breakdown and divorce from Harald, she had gone back to Salt Lake City with her "dads," who had come to rescue her. In her own eyes, this retreat and her divorce amount to a public admission of her private failure. Yet, a year or so later, she has the courage to return East to try once again to make good.

Her zealousness concerning World War II (caused possibly by her desire to best Harald who is an "America firster") leads to her death. Had she not been leaning out the window trying to identify planes, she would not have fallen and would not have died. The cigarette she left burning in the ashtray by her bedside, the radio still playing, and a forthcoming job interview point to the accidental nature of her fall; but this interpretation leaves unanswered the meaning of her death. If her fall is accidental, the question of learning is irrelevant. Then the group can be trusted when they agree, "How like Kay it was to have such violent preferences. . . . After all these years—seven, since graduation—the group could still remember exactly what she liked and what she despised. And she had never grown older and wiser" (356). Lakey buys an off-white silk gown for Kay to be buried in because she remembers that Kay had always longed for a Fortuny gown. Later, during the ceremony, Polly Andrews "thought of Kay's wedding and how young and superstitious they had all been that day and how little they had changed."

The group *cannot* recognize that Kay has developed or changed. To protect themselves, they must see her even in death as one of them, as unaware still of the failure of progress. But, if Kay's death were not accidental but purposeful, it can be assumed (following the line of reasoning in "Characters in Fiction" and dramatized in *A Charmed Life*) that, during the seven years encompassed in this novel, Kay had learned something and that, by so doing, she became mortal and moved out of the cast of comic or immortal characters. If this is the proper interpretation, Kay's nervous breakdown is what prepares her to learn by allowing her to face her failure. The knowledge she acquires, however, causes her to lose her balance or her perspective on herself and on the world. This theory makes her death as inevitable as Martha Sinnott's and dramatizes, as well, the foolishness of believing in the idea of progress. Again, the device of narrative mimicry offers little assistance in solving the problem of the author's intention.

After the funeral, Harald asks to ride with Lakey to the cemetery. The recognition that Lakey is a Lesbian has caused the group concern. Their initial response was bewilderment: "It occurred to them all that Lakey, who had always been frightening and superior, would now look down on them for not being Lesbians. On the other hand, she had seemed truly glad to see them" (370). However, Lakey's impeccableness soon modifies their apprehension; within a month, the group "accepts" her and the baroness. "Yet side by side with this the group felt, with one accord, that what had happened to Lakey was a tragedy. . . . They could not escape the gentle sense that the relationship these two had was perverted. One sign of this was the Baroness's jealousy" (372-73).

Although *The Group* ends with Lakey's apparent triumph over

Harald, her last laugh is not the signal of a victory. The match is a draw. No winner emerges. Life simply continues. When Lakey "tricks" Harald into exposing his hatred of "abnormality" by refusing to tell him whether she and Kay had ever been lovers, he turns on her (contradicting his earlier declaration of admiration) and accuses her angrily of being corrupt, parasitical, and un-American. He asks to be let out of the car, exclaiming, " 'You . . . bury her. You and the *group*' " (378). As Lakey drives away, she looks in the rear-view mirror and sees Harald cross the road and start to thumb a ride back to New York City. Such an ending is no triumph, only another one of Miss McCarthy's paradoxes, eternal and unanswerable. Harald's hitchhiking back to the City while the group moves away from him toward the cemetery represents neither progress nor solution—because there is no victory. At the end, there is only Lakey's voice saying that she is going to play a trick on Harald to revenge Kay and women: ". . . From her point of view, which he did not consider, poor normal Kay would not have sinned by being her prey instead of his. Far better for her, in fact, for Lakey, she hoped, would have been kind to her" (377). That raises again the problem of satire when handled through the device of narrative mimicry.

IV *Some Critical Reactions to* The Group

The Group is satire and not a realistic treatment of how a certain segment of society lived. Yet many readers have taken the realistic details at face value. Confusion of a contrary sort greeted the publication of *Gulliver's Travels* when an Irish bishop protested that he could not find a word of truth in the entire narrative. A good many of Miss McCarthy's readers refuse to disbelieve any of it—even Vassar girls! One vociferous member of the class of '17 advocates, "The College should repudiate author McCarthy and rescind her degree. It's been done before by other universities, and for far less injurious offenses. . . . What's become of the sanctity of marriage? Is there no love or beauty left in sex? Alumnae, we've been sold down the river! Vassar, make us proud again. Do *something*."[28] Another alumna writes, "I enjoyed the wit and fine writing of *The Group* and its excellent ear for conversation, but while I relished the wonderful description I missed any intimation of sympathy or compassion and felt that in its lack of depth and internal structure the book was more a piece of excellent journalism; an interim report rather than a novel."[29]

But wit, colloquial and anti-literary diction, and exacting descriptions of physical objects are the trappings not only "of excellent journalism" but of satire—in particular, the kind of satire that employs parody. To the extent that the writer of the mock heroic apes a style that is dignified and learned, so Mary McCarthy, writing a mock-chronicle, traces with infinite care the progress of her eight heroines and their friends. The details are painfully realistic—and sometimes tediously so—but in Miss McCarthy's relentless cataloging the mechanicalness and repetitiveness are basically comic. What makes *The Group* succeed as a mock-chronicle is the cumulative effect of its "histories" and the blatant stockpiling of its "facts."

But neither numbers and the accompanying lack of depth nor the painstaking attention to often picayune details and the resultant incongruity have proved sufficient to alert the unwary reader that *The Group* is something more—or less—than a novel. Why have such obvious signals failed to reveal a satiric intent behind the external, piecemeal realism of *The Group*? Part of the answer has to do with values. Mary McCarthy and her readers fail to see eye to eye; that is, her readers (including fellow alumnae of Vassar College) do not share Miss McCarthy's scrupulosity. Accordingly, they see Dottie as defamed and pitiful rather than as hilariously incongruous as she sits in Washington Square Park clutching the accoutrements of "love." And part of the answer goes back to the closed circuit of self-satire. Mary McCarthy is a member of the group—not as any one character but as a clever and not very secret sharer in their "Vassar-ness." But whereas some Vassar alumnae (and Vassar is nearly generic here) see only that Mary McCarthy has created an unflattering likeness of nine graduates of the class of '33, Miss McCarthy is able to hold herself at arm's length and laugh at some of her own foolish ways and enthusiasms—preferences that in themselves indicate a wrongness beyond the immediate object or advocate.

Critics looking for something nice to say about this novel have seized upon Polly Andrews. But the "goodness" of Polly does not indicate that Mary McCarthy is "mellowing." Any group of eight is bound to have its healthy apple. Besides, as in her earlier fiction, Miss McCarthy is in partial sympathy with what she satirizes. Vassar and the lure of "better things" are not so much to blame as the commerciality and ordinariness of the world and the eternal weakness of human nature that make the enlightened kneel before the false god of progress with as much alacrity as the uneducated masses with whom the "group" moves as a barely distinctive entity.

Significantly, the detailing of recipes, clothes, and furniture that occurs in *The Group* is the "drapery" that Mary McCarthy objects to in the fiction of other women novelists. As she relates in *The Paris Review* interview, she once had considered the possibility of writing an essay that would divide women writers into those representing "sense" and those standing for "sensibility." "I *am* for the ones who represent sense. . . ."[30] Aside from abetting the purpose of the mock-chronicle, the attention paid to drapery or to the material of sensibility underscores the element of sense that lifts *The Group* out of the category of "a trivial lady writer's novel" (to use Norman Podhoretz's phrase) and makes this work more than a period piece. In addition, as in her other works, externals are pressed into service as a way to judge people. For example, Dottie, coming into Dick Brown's room and noting its bare neatness, believes that she knows something about the man.

Norman Mailer praises Miss McCarthy for her sense of detail, which he considers "her single most impressive achievement"[31]— a left-handed compliment, to be sure, because Mailer also contends that *The Group* suffers from a lack of reach. "Her characters will come from one class and make no heroic journeys to other classes, they will not look to participate in the center of the history which is being made, and they will be the victim of no out-size passion."[32] In *The Group,* as in her other satirical fiction, Miss McCarthy has continued the practice of working within a relatively exclusive social milieu—in this instance within that segment of society for whom "the idea of progress" had some meaning. But once again, her narrowness of focus allows her to reproduce in realistic and accurate detail the world within the range of her vision.

A considerably more severe limitation on the effectiveness of *The Group* as satire is the ending which, as has been pointed out, is ironic (or paradoxical) rather than satiric. The responsibility for this shift in tone lies not only in the unresolved clash between Lakey and Harald but in the ambiguity surrounding the death of Kay Strong Petersen. As in *The Groves of Academe* and *A Charmed Life* in which emphasis on the character of Mulcahy and Martha and on a moral issue causes a movement away from satire, *The Group,* too, goes beyond the topical and the superficial to probe at something deep within the complex nature of man. Kay failed because she tried to realize her own ambition through Harald. But this is an error in judgment that sounds very nearly the note of tragedy, whether the person be a parent who tries to relive his life through a child or a teacher through a gifted pupil. For a person can realize himself only through the exercise of his own being. If Kay's death is a sign of her mortality and an indication that she has "learned," then these speculations are not simply fanciful, for she has the right to be considered as a serious heroine and not simply as a caricature. Of course, the significance of Kay's death remains a matter of conjecture, for the last word is the collective voice of the group and not that of Mary McCarthy.

In *The Paris Review* interview Mary McCarthy admitted that in her next work of fiction she would like to restore the author, for she believes that she has gone as far as she can in ventriloquism. "Because you find that if you obey this Jamesian injunction of 'Dramatize, dramatize,' and especially if you deal with comic characters, as in my case, there is so much you can't say because you're limited by these mentalities. It's just that a certain kind of intelligence . . . is more or less absent from the novel, and has to be, in accordance with these laws which the novel has made for itself."[33] In *Venice Observed* (1956) and in *The Stones of Florence* (1959), Miss McCarthy does speak in her own voice. In these books, of course, she moves out of fiction into a kind of reporting and analysis similar in many respects to some of the essays in *On the Contrary.*

CHAPTER 7

The Key That Works the City

A CITY, like a person, is a complex entity with an individuality of its own. In *Venice Observed* (1956) and *The Stones of Florence* (1959), Mary McCarthy approaches the two cities by adopting a device that had been used in the character sketches of *The Company She Keeps* and *Cast a Cold Eye*. As she "explained" Pflaumen in "The Genial Host" or Jim Barnett in "Portrait of the Intellectual as a Yale Man" by finding the key that worked them as individuals, so she "explains" Venice and Florence by finding the key that works each of these cities. In the character sketches, Miss McCarthy had discovered that externals (manner of dress, preference in foods, choice of friends, and so on) and knowledge of an individual's history (his heritage, place of origin, social position, education, and previous employment) provided her with ways of looking at a person and indicated a possible key to work the figure.

In *Venice Observed* and *The Stones of Florence*, Mary McCarthy adopts these same referents. History, although a complex and weird assortment of myth, actuality, and nineteenth-century sentimentalizing—particularly in the case of Florence, helps to explain the two cities. So do such obvious externals as the style of dress of the inhabitants, choice of home furnishings, characteristic businesses or industries, and recreational facilities. But the most useful key is preserved neither in the words nor deeds of man but in the semi-permanency of stone, canvas, and paint—in the buildings of Venice and Florence and the art treasures they store. In "The Cicerone," the two Americans in search of Europe believe that architecture is a key to a nation and to its people. "On the whole, architecture, they felt, provided the most solid answer to their social curiosity: the bedroom of Marie Antoinette at the Petit Trianon had informed them that the French royal family were dwarfs, a secret already hinted at in Mme Pompadour's bedroom at the Frick museum in New York. . . ."[1] But architecture, as they learn, is inadequate and even misleading.

In *Venice Observed* and *The Stones of Florence,* however, Mary McCarthy relies more heavily on architecture to explain each of the cities than she does on any other single aspect of man's achievement. In addition, architecture illustrates the central paradoxes upon which her analyses of Venice and Florence are built. Her fondness for paradoxes established itself first in the character sketches in *The Company She Keeps* and *Cast a Cold Eye.* But the key that works the figure in these sketches, however well it explains motives and actions, does not resolve the character; for a paradox, as Miss McCarthy has said, is eternal. Thus, while an understanding of what is paradoxical about Venice and Florence allows greater comprehension of the two cities, such knowledge does not resolve the complex nature of either city.

Miss McCarthy's seemingly accidental foray into the field of art history resulted from a suggestion on the part of Georges and Rosamond Bernier (publishers of *L'Oeil*) that she go to Venice and write a text for an art book. The success of *Venice Observed* (as the book jacket of *The Stones of Florence* relates) led to invitations from various publishers to do books on Yugoslavia, Poland, and Hungary. Miss McCarthy, however, turned down these offers in favor of writing about Florence. "Having learned, during three months in Venice, to sort out the Bellinis and the Vivarinis and the Tiepolos—she had supposed there was only one of each—she was determined to finish what she had started, to go back to the source, which was Florence, of the great Italian enlightenment."

Mary McCarthy has explained that she wrote both books very quickly, "the Venice one faster. Even the Florence book, with masses of research in it, was written very fast, with a great deal of energy, with a kind of liberated energy."[2] Although *Venice Observed* is written in the first person, she found this point of view no more restricting than the third person of *The Stones of Florence.* "I felt, you know, now I can talk freely. . . . And without the peculiar kind of painstakingness that's involved in the dramatization that one does in a novel, that is, when nothing can come in that hasn't been perceived through a character. The technical difficulties are so great, in projecting yourself, in feigning an alien consciousness, that too much energy gets lost, I think, in the masquerade."³ Also, the freedom from having to initiate and sustain a ventriloquial act in the travel books provided her with ample opportunity to pronounce absolute statements. And this she does, horrifying certain art historians by describing Michelangelo's figures of "Night" and "Day," "Twilight" and "Dawn" as "somewhat rubbery" or categorizing his architectural feats as "Brunelleschi, only more so." As well as speaking out freely in her own voice, Miss McCarthy gives vent to her enthusiasm for classifying. Folkway and ecclesiastical ceremony, countryside and city square, nobleman and church dignitary, artist and shopkeeper—each is identified and labeled. Although neither *Venice Observed* nor *The Stones of Florence* is a large book (each is roughly forty-five thousand words), both are catalogues of facts, observations, anecdotes, analogies, and judgments.

Venice Observed and *The Stones of Florence* differ rather sharply in tone and format. The Venice book is livelier than the later work and manages (a result, in part, of the first-person point of view) to bring the reader into what becomes an act of discovery. Venice is "discovered"—or observed; Florence is lectured on—or explained (and even moralized about). In *Venice Observed*, an appendix contains "Comments on Venetian Civilization" and "Notes on the Plates" by André Chastel. In *The Stones of Florence*, Mary McCarthy is her own art historian, and her text carries the total burden of fact that the *Venice Observed* appendix in part assumes. Since André Chastel's "Notes on the Plates" obviously follow the sequence of plates in the text, and since that ordering is chronological, the appendix provides a brief history of Venetian art, architecture, and customs. This arrangement allows Miss McCarthy greater freedom in the text, with the result that *Venice Observed* is also more journalistic in tone than *The Stones of Florence*.

Although the present serves as a frame in both *Venice Observed* and *The Stones of Florence*, the drift of the text in the two works is chronological. Much backtracking occurs, however, and in the Venice book especially there is considerable interplay between the past and the present day. Unlike the strictly chronological ordering of the photographs in *Venice Observed*, there is an attempt to make the illustrations in *The Stones of Florence* correspond to the text. This ordering contributes to the sometimes startling effectiveness of the 128 black and white photographs that are the work chiefly of Evelyn Hofer. Succinctly and dramatically, they underscore an observation or prove a point. Unlike Venice, Florence is austere and masculine. "It stands four-square and direct, with no air of mystery, no blandishments, no furbelows—no Gothic lace or baroque swirls. Against the green Arno, the ocher-and-dun file of hotels and palazzi has the spruce, spare look of a regiment drawn up in drill order."[4] The black and white and grays of the photographs illustrate well the severity of the Florence described in the text and make the twelve color plates appear inconsequential and unsuitable. *Venice Observed,* in contrast, abounds in color photographs of the city and its art treasures. But color is very important to Venice, and the photographs, by capturing the opulence and burnishing and gleaming of the jeweled mosaics and the multi-colored, lavishly ornamented façades of the buildings, surround the reader with the charm and glitter of this city.

The differences that mark *Venice Observed* and *The Stones of Florence* serve as an objective correlative to the actual contrasts that exist between the two cities. As depicted by Miss McCarthy, appearance is reality in Venice and the tourist Venice is the real Venice. In Florence, reality is partially obscured by appearance, and the "actual" Florence is missed by the unselective and unperceptive tourist. Consequently, Venice can be observed, but Florence has to be interpreted.

I   *Venice Described*

Venice Observed begins with quotations from Herbert Spencer and Michel de Montaigne, both of whom were disappointed by the actual Venice. Although neither of these men is noted for his sensitivity to art, both are rationalists and Mary McCarthy uses their opinions to bolster her judgment that the rationalist mind has always doubted Venice. "This grossly advertised wonder, this gold idol with clay feet, this *trompe-l'oeil,* this painted deception, this cliché—what intelligent iconoclast could fail to experience a destructive impulse in her presence?"[5] But Venice triumphs over the "dry, prose people of superior intelligence" as she enjoys and even "uses" the tourists that have flocked into her confines since the early eighteenth century.

Although Venice boasts an exotic resplendence, the Venetians themselves were "a commercial people who lived solely for gain." A contradiction seems to exist between the venality of the citizenry and what Mary McCarthy describes as the fairy-tale loveliness of their city. But the paradox becomes understandable by analyzing the images of beauty in fairy-tales. "They are images of money. Gold, caskets of gold, caskets of silver, the miller's daughter spinning gold all night long . . . the cave of Ali Baba stored with stolen gold and silver, the underground garden in which Aladdin found jewels growing on trees. . . ." These are the elements of Venetian art. "A wholly materialist city is nothing but a dream incarnate. Venice is the world's unconscious: a miser's glittering hoard . . ." (50).

But another, deeper contradiction exists that cannot be so summarily dismissed. And that also has to do with the fairy-tale irrationality of Venice. "Venetian architecture is characterized by the unvarying importance given to the buildings' exteriors, to the façades conceived as integral parts of the monumental unity of a square or a canal" (Appendix, 188). The lack of interest in the backs of buildings causes Venice to appear unattractive when viewed in the round. "Venetian architecture . . . is stage architecture, caring little (up to Palladio) for principles and concerned mainly with 'effects.' Venice is the world's loveliest city, but it produced only one architect—Palladio—who worked along conceptual lines" (113).

The persistent theme of *Venice Observed* has to do with the fraudulent nature of Venice, symbolized by the fondness of the Venetians for mirrors and masks and supported by the observation that Venice is constructed of "stolen merchandise." A totally improbable city, it peers into the somewhat pocked surfaces of the canals to affirm the reality of its existence: "It is the same reassurance that a looking-glass offers us: the guarantee that we are real" (160). Not surprisingly, therefore, the rationalist mind objects to all this trumpery and to feeling what one is "supposed to feel, in the presence of marvels."

Yet the Venetians, as Mary McCarthy describes them, were extraordinarily rational. So was their Republic, "a wholly rational structure" with "no interest in reason in its purer forms—only in *applied* reason, as one might say applied science. The subtle Venetian intelligence expended itself in diplomatic '*relazioni*' and practical statecraft" (83). The ideal citizen of this ideal Republic was "reasonable, peaceful, avid only for consumption, unsuperstitious . . ." (66). The Venetian character was firmly rooted in the possible and the tangible. Yet, in the face of this reasonableness, the Venetians created a city that delights by excess, a city built where a city should not be—on water, a city that is a magician's trick and an artist's palette—in short, a city that is irrational.

Conversely, the Florentines, who were incapable of governing themselves well and who existed almost constantly in a state of martial strife, built a city that is an embodiment of reason, moderation, and tranquility. "The strong drama of Florentine life seems to have resulted, with Brunelleschi, in an art of perfect balance. The terrible struggles that took place in this city and in which the Pazzi family, a little later, took such a part had their reward in equilibrium—a reconciliation of forms" (*The Stones of Florence*, 73). This paradox is implicit in the juxtaposing of images and events in *Venice Observed* and *The Stones of Florence*.

Mary McCarthy describes present-day Venice by utilizing the person and habits of her landlady, "a tall ash-blond stringbean of a woman, with a long, droll Modigliani face—a good-natured, feckless comedian. . . . a true daughter of Venice . . ." (28-29). The apartment, consisting of four large rooms that overlook the garden of a palazzo, is pleasantly "furnished, for the most part, in a gay Venetian rococo, blue-and-white stripes, pink rosebuds, cabinets painted in the manner of Tiepolo, chairs with scallop-shell backs." The only drawback to this seemingly fine arrangement is the signora (separated from her husband for "tax purposes," so the real estate agent assures Miss McCarthy) and her two children (only one had been specified in the original invoice) who live upstairs and share their downstairs tenant's bathtub and the common entrance hall. Almost immediately, Miss McCarthy discovers that the signor ("too coarse-grained and swart to be a real Venetian") beds down nightly with his wife. But only the sound of his footsteps or his matutinal arguments signify his presence. ". . . That is all he is to me: a stormy, uxorious voice, a whisk of moustache and coat-tails, a surreptitious step on the stair. Like Jove, he visits his premises by stealth, and I come to think of him as simply a male totem, a bull or a shower of coins" (28).

The Venetians, in the custom of seafaring men, are fond of pets, particularly cats. "The signora has a cat, I discover, from hearing it claw at my windows, trying to get in. Its persistence tells me that it must live here, though the signora does not at first confess this. It is another displaced person, like the signor, and has been put out to live on the roof-tiles during the period when the apartment is rented" (33). Two goldfish, although allowed to remain in the downstairs kitchen, lead even more pitiable existences. Lethargic and blanched, they live on a chemical generated by the interaction of the aquarium water and the five- and ten-lire pieces that line the bottom of the bowl (the signora refuses to feed them or to put any greenery into the aquarium). A good square meal of fish food, Miss McCarthy knows, would kill the starving fish; but she does not act because she is unwilling to annoy the signora, who is proud of the cleverness of her savings-bank aquarium and of the tenacious staying power of the goldfish. "So I conclude that I had best leave them as they are and take them as an allegory on Venice, a society which lived in a bowl and drew its sustenance from the filth of lucre. Once flame-colored, today it is a little pale and moribund, like the fish after two years of the signora's regimen" (37).

In the last chapter, Mary McCarthy again takes up the signora and her family who, with the elapsing of time, have resumed partial possession of the downstairs apartment, picking over her belongings in her absence and watching her when she cooks. "It is their curiosity, I feel, that leads them to try out all sorts of dodges on me—merely to test my reactions. . . . Their whole life seems to be conducted on a similar principle; there is a continuous testing of reality, to see how far it will yield and when it will resist—Venetian experimentation" (165-66). And so Miss McCarthy tolerates the petty, transparent deceits of the signora and her bizarre dealings with tradespeople. In the mysteriousness of her business transactions, the signora is similar to Mr. Sheer in "Rogue's Gallery" (*The Company She Keeps*). Unlike Mr. Sheer, however, the function of her many deceptions is not to command belief. "She is an utter realist who lives in a web of unreal schemes and plans that can never come off. . . . She is always Venice in her own eyes, fallen on evil days, reduced to living on the foreigner, who will soon go away and leave her. But she does not really care; she is a fatalist" (170-71).

Between and around the descriptions of the signora are a history of Venice and a catalogue of Venetian artists and art objects. Symbolic of Venice, in the way the Duomo of Brunelleschi represents Florence, is St. Mark's. Begun in the ninth century to house the body of Saint Mark (stolen by two Venetian merchants in 828 from Alexandria), the edifice was burned in 976 and restored shortly thereafter. But, toward the middle of the eleventh century, "the Republic wanted a more impressive basilica in keeping with its growing power. In 1063, Doge Domenico Contarini began work on the new St. Mark's, having chosen as model one of the most venerated sanctuaries of the East, the famous Church of the Holy Apostles in Constantinople" (Appendix, 185).

As well as symbolizing the Roman-Byzantine heritage of Venice (and it is the Eastern influence that is largely responsible for the exotic strain in Venetian art and architecture), St. Mark's illustrates the Venetians' habit of looting and the excellent use to which they put their booty. The materials to build St. Mark's came principally from the remains of early Christian temples and basilicas and from old, abandoned monuments on the mainland. The ornaments used in decorating the interior were brought back, for the most part, from Eastern cities. Indeed, Mary Mc-Carthy finds that the special art of the Venetians lay in their blending and grouping diverse elements—a conglomeritic art that gives St. Mark's the outward appearance of "an Oriental pavilion—half pleasure-house, half war-tent, belonging to some great satrap. Inside, glittering with jewels and gold, faced with precious Eastern marbles, jasper and alabaster, porphyry and verd-antique, sustained by Byzantine columns in the same materials, of varying sizes and epochs, scarcely a pair alike, this dark cruciform cave has the look of a robber's den" (43).

Venice, unlike Florence, has its humorous side; it is "a kind of pun on itself, which is another way of saying that it is a mirror held up to its own shimmering image—the central conceit on which it has evolved" (20). Miss McCarthy points out that a very noticeable twinning characterizes Venice. Duplicates or near duplicates of buildings, statuary, and paintings occur. Even the artists themselves come in pairs or trios; for example, there are three Bellinis, three Vivarinis, two Tintorettos, two Longhis, two Tiepolos, two Guardis, and so on. "These painting 'firms'—and there were family firms of sculptors also—were something unique in Italy, at least on such a scale. *Bellini and Sons, Tintoretto and Son, Longhi and Son,* reliable companies turning out a high-quality brand product, like the jewelers and glassblowers, proclaim the business-like character, the conservatism, of Venetian civilization" (115). Exaggerated and improbable, Venice "*is* another world, a palpable fiction, in which the unexpected occurs with regularity; that is why it hovers on the brink of humor" (25). In the make-believe atmosphere of Venice, the events and objects of this world become humorous by revealing their essential absurdity. A traffic light over a canal intersection—necessary or not—looks slightly foolish.

The cataloguing of Venice continues. *Venice Observed* is a compendium of information, a treasure-house similar in some respects to St. Mark's—filled with borrowed facts and lavishly ornamented but nonetheless a work of art because of the singular blending of the diverse elements and the uniqueness of the animating vision. *Venice Observed* contains snatches of history from the beginnings of the Republic as a refuge from Attila in the fifth century, through the days of Venice's glory as a maritime power, to the fall of the Republic at the end of the eighteenth century; comments on the artists and their work, from Paolo Veneziano to the Bellinis, Carpaccio, Giorgione, Titian, Lorenzo Lotto, Tintoretto, Matteo Pagan, Veronese, the Tiepolos, Canaletto, Pietro Longhi, and Francesco Guardi; an explanation of the governmental workings of the Republic, including a description of the complex method of "electing" the doge; an account of Torcello and Burano and Chioggia (present and past); and much more.

Venice Observed is the collected observations of one person concerning a city about which everything that can be said has been said, a city where the "crafts have become sideshows—glassblowing, bead-stringing, lace-making . . ."; a city of twice-told tales—the ducal bonnet, the Inquisitors, the Doge's golden umbrella, the Marriage of the Adriatic, the Bridge of Sighs, Casanova, Shylock, the Rialto, the pigeons, Marco Polo, Byron,

Wagner, and "finally, last and first, the gondola, the eternal gondola, with its steel prow and its witty gondolier. . . ."

II *Florence Explained*

The road to Venice, for Mary McCarthy, led to Florence, because "everything in Venice, in Italy for that matter, really points to Florence, everything in the Renaissance anyway, like signposts on a road."[6] As well as being more scholarly than *Venice Observed, The Stones of Florence* has a didacticism that is absent from the earlier book. "I felt that through the medium of writing about this city I could set forth what I believed in, what I was for; that through this city, its history, its architects and painters—more its sculptors than its painters—it was possible for me to say what I believed in. And say it very affirmatively, even though this all ended in 1529. . . ."[7]

In her other writing (both in the essays and in the fiction), it is apparent that to Miss McCarthy truthfulness constitutes a criterion by which a work of art, a political action, or even a marriage can be judged. Unquestionably, the importance to Miss McCarthy of honesty and her own efforts to be honest predispose her toward Florence and such virtues as "the wise division of space, substantiality, simplicity, economy, and restraint"—and against Venice and the untruthfulness of façades and exaggerated ornamentation (although, as always, she is intrigued by the mysterious and slightly fraudulent). Also, she sees in Brunelleschi, the artist-hero of *The Stones of Florence*, a clarity of mind and a definiteness of purpose that contrast sharply with the irrationality of the modern world and its economy of conspicuous consumption. Ironically, the Florence of mass tourism pays little respect to Brunelleschi. The first chapter describes contemporary Florence:

> Florence is scraping the bottom of the tourist barrel. And the stolid presence of these masses with their polyglot guides in the Uffizi, in the Pitti, around the Baptistery doors and the Medici Tombs, in the cell of Savonarola and the courtyard of Palazzo Vecchio is another of the "disagreeables," as the Victorians used to call them, that have made Florence intolerable and, more than that, inexplicable to the kind of person for whom it was formerly a passion. (4)

Florence is the antithesis of Venice in many ways. The exterior of the palazzi "bristle like fortresses or dungeons, and, to the passing tourist, their thick walls and bossy surfaces seem to repel the very notion of hospitality. . . . The Florentine palaces . . . hide their private life like misers, which in fact the Florentines are reputed to be" (5). Also, unlike Venice, the workaday city of Florence does not cater to tourists. "Tourism, in a certain sense, is an accidental by-product of the city—at once profitable and a nuisance, adding to the noise and the congestion, raising prices for the population" (10). Although Florence has very little heavy industry, small crafts and trades flourish. Among Florentine manufactures are furniture, gloves, shoes, handbags, luggage, textiles, table linens, chemicals, optical equipment, and wrought iron. The unwillingness of the Florentines to exhibit their city to foreigners (another trait which sets them apart from the Venetians) and the grouping of the touristic parties at such places as the Medici Chapel allow the selective visitor, however, to spend

> an hour, two hours, in the great churches of Brunelleschi—Santo Spirito and San Lorenzo—and no one will speak to you or pay you any heed. . . . The smaller churches—Santa Trinita, Santa Felicita, Ognissanti, Santissima Annunziata, Santa Maria Maddalena dei Pazzi, San Giovannino dei Cavalieri—are rarely visited; neither is the Pazzi Chapel outside Santa Croce, and the wonderful Giottos, freshly restored, in the Bardi Chapel of Santa Croce. . . . (13)

And it is these parts of Florence that please Miss McCarthy and negate the hot, mosquito-ridden summers and the severely damp winters; the surliness of waiters and the overpriced, unappealing food; and the din and the dangers of the traffic-laden streets.

Each of the following chapters, although seemingly composed of fragments, defines Florence in various ways by concentrating on a particular aspect of Florentine art or history. And, as in *Venice Observed*, the basically chronological movement of the chapters provides a brief history of the city from its beginnings as a Roman outpost (legend erroneously attributes the founding of Florence to Caesar as a prelude to the capture of Fiesole) to the "tooled-leather" Florence of the Victorians. Particular attention is given to the history of Florence during the period described in Dante's *Divine Comedy* and to the issues involved in the quarrels between the Guelphs and the Ghibellines. Stingy, envious, and proud (Miss McCarthy translates Dante), the Florentines of the Middle Ages and the Renaissance were fiercely independent and possessed by "a determination to be outdone by no one. This, all the old chroniclers agree, was the cause of their civic turmoils: a boundless ambition and its corollary, an overweening envy" (38).

Miss McCarthy devotes much space to discussing the statuary which, she believes, embodies the genius or attendant spirit of Florence and "is part of the very fabric of the city—the *respublica* or public thing. It belongs to a citizenry, stubborn and independent, and to a geography, like that of Athens, of towering rock and stone. The Florentine sculptors of the *quattrocento* sprang from the quarries of the neighboring hills, where the *macigno* or gray *pietra serena* was cut." The colors of Florence—white, black, gray, dun, and bronze—are the colors of metal and stone, the primitive elements of the Stone Age, the Bronze Age, the Iron Age. "The hammer and the chisel strike the somber music of Florentine art and architecture, of the Florentine character" (20). In the judgment of Miss McCarthy, the extinction of the Republic and the flourishing of Florentine humanism—conditions which gave rise to the veneration of the antique and to the appearance of the connoisseur—marked the end of the heroic age of sculpture and the beginning of the slavish imitation of classical models. "Naturally, in none of this statuary . . . is there a grain of that local tender piety, religious or civic, that appears in its purest, most intense concentration in Donatello's figures." Donatello, Mary McCarthy affirms, was "the most numinous of all the Florentine sculptors, and Michelangelo, though bigger, was not as fine" (27). In Michelangelo, she senses a straining and tenseness in the knotted muscles of his suffering forms: "He anticipated the baroque, a style utterly un-Florentine, whose power center was papal Rome" (28).

Miss McCarthy credits the Florentines with having "invented the Renaissance, which is the same as saying that they invented the modern world—not, of course, an unmixed good. Florence was a turning-point. . . ." The reflective visitor in Florence today, Miss McCarthy explains, is often troubled by "the feeling that a terrible mistake was committed here, at some point between Giotto and Michelangelo, a mistake that had to do with power and megalomania or gigantism of the human ego" (64). But the greatness of Florentine art could not be stopped at Masaccio's "Trinity" or Donatello's "San Giorgio" or Giotto's bell tower. The dynamism that the Florentines introduced into the arts involved "a continuous process of acceleration, a speed-up, which created obsolescence around it, as new methods do in industry. The *last word*, throughout the Renaissance, always came from Florence" (65). But the "last word" was, in some instances, the "first word," for Florentines are responsible for the first important literary work in the vulgar tongue (Dante); the discovery of perspective and the raising of the first massive dome since antiquity (Brunelleschi); the first opera (Jacopo Peri); the first public library (founded by Cosimo il Vecchio in the convent of San Marco); the first literary criticism in the modern sense (Boccaccio's lectures on the *Divine Comedy*); a pioneer study on the principles of political science (Machiavelli); and the first modern art criticism (L. B. Alberti).

The discovery of the principles of ordered recession to create an illusion of depth was, for the artists of that period, more than a technique that would assure them of attaining correct proportions in their paintings. "It was an eerie marvel, a mystery, partaking of the uncanny; to a nature like Uccello's, it had all the charm of magic" (49). The vanishing point exercised a spell like that of the horizon toward which Columbus and his mariners sailed. In contrast to the Venetians who, for centuries, never tired of "the deception of feigned marble, feigned brocade, fictive doors and windows, false vistas," the Florentines were intrigued by space and the greater honesty that perspective would allow. "Their civic halls, churches, and dwellings were too real for games of make-believe" (57).

Bigness, Miss McCarthy points out, is one of the forms that beauty can take, a principle well understood by the artists and craftsmen of the Renaissance who equated magnitude with sublimity and daring. In 1296, the first of the great Florentine master builders, Arnolfo, was commissioned to begin work on the Duomo (Santa Maria del Fiore). But, before the roof could be put over the enormous expanse of the tribune, Arnolfo died and left behind him an architectural problem that was not to be solved for more than a hundred years. No precedent was available to follow, for the methods used successfully by the ancients were not known.

In 1420, Brunelleschi, in response to a competition, settled the issue by announcing that he had "found a way of raising the dome of Santa Maria del Fiore without supports—a thing everyone believed to be impossible" (70). The dome that Brunelleschi erected, by means of a double cupola (one shell resting on another inside it—an idea he had probably got from studying the Pantheon), in addition to being a structural triumph, was also practical, with rain gutters, ducts to reduce wind pressure, inside iron hooks for scaffolding, and so on. A tremendous undertaking, the Duomo still astonishes by its massiveness.

In the purity and simplicity of Brunelleschi, Miss McCarthy declares, "the Florentine tradition reached its highest point" (72). Brunelleschi wins her praise because she considers his work truthful: "All great Florentine art, from Giotto through the *quattrocento,* has the faculty of amazing with its unexpected and absolute truthfulness. This faculty was once called beauty" (76). Michelangelo was always conscious of Brunelleschi's greatness; and, when called upon to do the dome of St. Peter's, he paid a tribute to Brunelleschi with a rhyming couplet which, translated, reads, "I am going to make its sister,/Bigger, yes, but not more beautiful." And, in Miss McCarthy's judgment, the dome of St. Peter's is no more beautiful than Brunelleschi's, for Michelangelo, in whom the Florentine passion for greatness went beyond all human limits, could only surpass Brunelleschi by being more excessive. "Among living competitors, he would accept only God for his rival, and his late, lumbering, unfinished works are all metaphors for the primal act of bringing shape out of chaos" (79). This refusal to set boundaries around his ambition caused him to leave many works unfinished because of the impossibility of executing his supra-human conceptions.

Miss McCarthy finds that in Florentine painting as in politics two distinct strains existed: "One is stern, majestic, autumnal, sometimes harsh or livid—the Guelphish painting" that began with Giotto and continued with such artists as Orcagna, Masaccio, Uccello, Andrea del Castagno, Antonio Pollaiuolo, Leonardo, and Michelangelo. The other strain is "sweet, flowery, springlike—Ghibelline painting that seeded in from Siena and blossomed first in Bernardo Daddi, then in Fra Angelico and the little masters who followed him, next in Fra Filippo, Verrocchio, and, finally, Botticelli" (82). The Guelphish works portray the stony city of Florence but the countryside in May appears in the Ghibelline. As well as discussing the set of painters that belong to Maytime Florence (upon whose work the popular idea of Florence rests), Miss McCarthy discusses the Mannerist painters of the sixteenth century, in particular Il Rosso Fiorentino and Jacopo Pontormo. Although Miss McCarthy finds early Florentine Mannerism "twitching, hag-ridden, agoraphobic," she credits the Florentine Mannerists with being "the first to feel the strain and hollowness of the *cinquecento*" (113).

Despite the failure of Florentine painting and sculpture to recover from their collapse in the middle of the sixteenth century (and nowhere in this work is Miss McCarthy's bias so openly and emphatically stated as in the last chapter), Florence did not turn into a dream as did Venice or petrify like Siena, Rimini, Mantua, or Ravenna. Unlike these other cities, Florence survived because of its crafts, out of which its art had initially grown; and the last chapter closes with a discussion of present-day Florence. Of particular interest to Mary McCarthy is the Florentine method of restoration—less drastic than that practiced in London and New York and "one of the new wonders of the art world" (118). In the exactingness of this delicate repair work, she finds a symbol for the thriftiness and efficiency that is one side of the complex character of the Florentines.

III   *Some Critical Reactions*

Critics have not been altogether pleased with Mary McCarthy's insistence on linking the demise of the heroic age of Florentine sculpture and architecture and painting with the fall of the Republic and the final arrival of the Medici. Such a construct is very admirable and democratic, they say, but not true to the facts. Miss McCarthy, the reviewer of the *Times Literary Supplement* argues, has fallen prey to the democratic fallacy that the history of Florence and Florentine culture closes with the fall of the Republic—a bias that makes her neglect the many works of consequence done under Cosimo I and his successors.

"The evidence of this is still all over Florence, but because Miss McCarthy and the sixteenth century do not hit it off, we are asked to shut our eyes and make believe it is not there."[8]

However narrow Miss McCarthy's interpretation of the art of the *cinquecento* may be and however selective she is in picking examples of that art for discussion, she does not *neglect* the period. She simply chooses to see what she wants to in this century. And, in her estimation, the art of this period is untruthful and private when compared with that of the previous two centuries. Mary McCarthy, it must never be forgotten, *admires* truthfulness. Thus (and this is an oversimplification) she admires the art produced during the *quattrocento* and the Republic because she considers this art honest; and she dislikes the *cinquecento* and the Medici because, in her vision, the Medicis were responsible for stifling the spirit of human freedom that allowed such artists as Donatello, Uccello, and Brunelleschi to flourish. As a result, the art of the sixteenth century is, in general, manneristic and pretentious. Linking the fall of the Republic with the end of Florence's greatness as a begetter of honest and vital artists is a form of intellectual bias; but, for Miss McCarthy, it springs from her basic need to sort the truthful from the untruthful. As well as affording *The Stones of Florence* an internal consistency, this point of view permits her to make a statement about man and perfectibility, and it also gives the book a singularity and a shape that distinguishes it from the mass of other books that have been written about Florence—a city that has intrigued the imaginations of men for more than six centuries. Once again, as in the essays and drama reviews, Mary McCarthy is speaking in her own voice and pronouncing absolute statements with unabashed gusto. And her individual perception makes *Venice Observed* and *The Stones of Florence* significant or, to use an overused word, *truthful* in terms of their conception and intention.

CHAPTER 8

The Proper Study

MARY McCARTHY in *Theatre Chronicles* conjectured that quite possibly Ibsen's most important contribution as a playwright is clinical. He was the first, she observed, to put a neurotic woman—and she cites as examples Hedda, Ellida Wangel, Mrs. Solness, Nora—on the stage.[1] In a sense, the most important contribution of Mary McCarthy to literature is clinical. Her fiction is a pioneer study in a temper that can be defined— for want of a more precise phrase—as Eastern-Urban. What makes her accomplishment more significant is that she writes about the urban intelligentsia without the tie that binds—even if it exists to be broken—Jewishness of a Saul Bellow and without the "hipsterism" of a Norman Mailer. But describing the Eastern-Urban temper is a not altogether rewarding task.

Intellectuals and quasi-intellectuals (particularly the latter) are a talkative lot—theory people who believe in causes but who are constitutionally unable, for the most part, to put ideas into action. *The Oasis* dramatizes this dilemma. Indeed, it is difficult to imagine a worse torment for the characters in a novel by Mary McCarthy than to conceive of their being deprived suddenly and absolutely of the power to speak.

Also, the relative unimportance of the family in the urbanized East contributes to Mary McCarthy's focusing on a collective protagonist in *The Oasis* and in *The Group* and emphasizing acquaintances—persons peripheral to the heroine—in *The Company She Keeps,* in *Cast a Cold Eye,* and in *A Charmed Life.* Children are seldom heard and only occasionally seen, the most glaring exceptions being the snotty-nosed, damp-bottomed off- spring of Mulcahy in *The Groves of Academe* and the sons of Priss and Norine in *The Group,* who exist more as theories than

as real children. Even the humor in the writing of Mary Mc-
Carthy is bookish, witty rather than slapstick, ironic rather than
side-splitting. Jokes that are allusions to literature, deliberate
folksy colloquialisms incongruous to the speaker, plays on words,
syntactical confusion and errors in quoting from learned sources,
repetition, and exaggeration provide the comic elements in her
fiction.

Miss McCarthy's penchant to "explain" is also a somewhat
Northern characteristic. A writer like Eudora Welty is content
to describe what is mysterious about human beings and the way
they act. But this approach is not for Mary McCarthy to whom
mysteries are a challenge that demand clarification. Working
from the premise that effects must have causes, she sets out to
discover *why* man acts as he does, to find the "key," and to
classify the person or event that has baffled her intelligence.
Often, however, the "key" is a paradox that defies resolution by
its eternality. For human nature is a complex mechanism. The
intricate parts can be examined and their functions understood.
But even working from the inside out, neither Mary McCarthy
nor any other writer can go beyond exposing and explaining the
odd and contradictory behavior of man. Such explanations, however, are simply another way of describing what is mysterious
about human nature. The mystery *is* the contradiction itself.

Another characteristic of the Eastern-Urban temper is an apparent indifference to nature. Most often, of course, characters in
such fiction move against the background of the metropolis. But
Mary McCarthy chooses to ignore nature and to concentrate on
man and his ideas even in *The Oasis, The Groves of Academe,*
and *A Charmed Life*—works in which the countryside provides
a milieu. But man without nature (or God—the principle of a
Creator serves the same purpose) can lose sight rapidly of his
finiteness and imperfectibility devoid of an omniscient power
that allows a distancing. In *The Oasis,* when Katy Norell realizes
her own imperfectibility and declares that "her hunger for goodness was an appetency not of this world and not to be satisfied
by actions, which would forever cheat its insistencies,"[2] she is
uttering the eternally despairing cry of the typical Mary Mc-
Carthy heroine and of Mary McCarthy herself. And in this situation bookishness is of no help. In fact, the "good" characters in
the fiction of Miss McCarthy tend to confuse themselves with

literary images and to accept as attainable highly idealized values and goals.

The strongly idealized standards that Mary McCarthy sets for herself and her fellow men are responsible in part for her own highly censorious attitude—a trait that she shares with the urban intelligentsia. But what isolates Miss McCarthy from such writers and people is that she criticizes herself *first* and then "others." The truthfulness that she values so highly prevents her from saying that to be almost good is to be "good enough" or from being satisfied with words that have only a tangential relationship to reality. Accordingly, she views critically the discrepancy between appearance and reality. The vehicle she chooses to dramatize this incongruity is satire.

I *Concerning Satire*

The decadence of Rome caused Juvenal to remark, "It is difficult *not* to write satire." Discussing the "irreality" of the post-Hiroshima world in "The Fact in Fiction," Mary McCarthy points out that the finite world of the novelist and of ordinary man has been rendered not only insignificant but "improbable" and "unveracious" by such recent events as Auschwitz, the hydrogen bomb, and space satellites—occurrences in themselves that "stagger belief." Very possibly, Mary McCarthy has chosen to reply in kind, that is, to mock back at a world that has become in her eyes fantastic and to fight "irreality" with "irreality." The distorting mirror of satire provides an appropriate means for the human intelligence to respond to absurdity. Like Juvenal, but for different motivation, Mary McCarthy is compelled to write satirically because of what she sees in the external world that lies about her.

As noted previously, Miss McCarthy has acknowledged that although she would like to write like Tolstoy and imagines that her vision of the world parallels with some exactness what Tolstoy saw, "my pen or my typewriter simply balks; it 'sees' differently from me and records what to me, as a person, are distortions and angularities." In *The Paris Review* interview she has admitted to writing "on the bias" as a result of "seeing things with a sort of swerve and swoop." Mary McCarthy, then, may be very much like Horace who once said that he wrote satires because he could not write epics. Very probably, Miss McCarthy writes as she does because technically she cannot write any other way, that is, when she tries to write fiction the result is *A Charmed Life* (of all her "novels" the one that most resembles a novel) instead of an *Anna Karenina*.

Another possible motive to explain *why* Mary McCarthy chooses to write satirically may be found in the words of Byron: "And if I laugh at any mortal thing,/'Tis that I may not weep." Instead of despairing at the eternal foolishness of man, Miss McCarthy, like Byron, laughs. The wit is defensive, a way of dealing with disillusionment. Without question, the satirical fiction of Mary McCarthy is the result of her particular vision and her particular gifts. As pointed out in Chapter V, to insist that satire *must* seek to bring about reform through ridicule is to cling to a definition basically untenable. It is enough if satire ridicules— gently or harshly but always with wit—and thereby exposes the follies of man to laughter even though it does not necessarily laugh man out of those follies. One feels that Mary McCarthy knows that the latter is an impossible task.

Wyndham Lewis, who argues strongly against the assumption that all satire must be moralistic, affirms that the true subject of art is the external, the plastic surface of things. Satire, he states, is pre-eminently an art of what might be termed the "outside." Mary McCarthy has a good eye and a good ear for the details of the external world. Part of her considerable success in describing "plastic surfaces" stems from her familiarity with what she is satirizing, a familiarity that results from identification and participation. But, beneficial as such first-hand knowledge is, satire directed against the values and the milieu that have sustained one's life is on ethical grounds somewhat suspect and for esthetic reasons partially disadvantageous.

The principal drawback to the kind of self-satire that Mary McCarthy writes is that she cannot oppose too strongly what she exposes to ridicule, for a basic sympathy commits her irrefutably to what she is satirizing. Various motives can be ascribed to what drives a person to satirize himself. One has to do with a desire to seek protection from the ridicule of others (a concern evident in *Memories of a Catholic Girlhood*). Making fun of oneself is a way of beating others to the punch. Another reason stems from the honesty that prevents Mary McCarthy from glossing over her own failures. But because she is a curiously objective writer despite the subjectivity of her material, she treats her short-comings humorously. Still another reason is that she apparently cannot stop being her own central idea—even satirically. Along with not being able to oppose too strongly, this kind of satire does not allow Mary McCarthy to make clear what standards the institutions or persons she is ridiculing have failed to meet. For example, almost all her readers, despite their lack of homogeneity, would agree that the pedagogy of Jocelyn College is confused and ineffective. But what values are better than those that Jocelyn represents?

Such a question does not demand that Miss McCarthy suggest a way of reform. But ridicule by implying a wrongness implies also the existence of a rightness or of a positive force. The failure of Mary McCarthy to stand apart ethically from what she satirizes leaves unstated the contrary principle or, more specifically, *what* is wrong. Unless, of course, Miss McCarthy simply assumes that her readers would know that the unstated "positive" assumption upon which she bases her criticism is also the impossible—the realization of perfectibility in men pure in heart and deed. And esthetically, the device of narrative mimicry offers no clarification. By disappearing into her characters and thereby ruling out her own voice from the novel, Mary McCarthy cannot step in to clarify her values.

For these reasons, what is satiric in her fiction becomes at the conclusion of her novels a surprisingly mild-mannered exposure of the weakness of human nature, the kind of weakness that makes Vassar girls stoop for progress, utopias collapse, progressive colleges run afoul, and artists' colonies prove destructive to those who wish to live by reason. And, because Mary McCarthy is dealing with intellectuals, she seems to be saying that knowledge is little help. Man can learn, yes, but he can change his ways only externally; he cannot become perfect or even better than he is because of the inherent and insurmountable flaws of human nature.

This point of view is, of course, virulently anti-Socratic. Knowledge, Miss McCarthy has dramatized, is neither a virtue nor a safeguard. Such a position is close to that of Swift and Voltaire, for both these men depicted the impotence of reason; Candide, by leaving the bland reasonableness of Eldorado; Gulliver, by rejecting the sterile rationality of the Houyhnhnms. Reason is, after all, only one aspect of human nature, although it is a large one because man *is* a rational animal. But the other aspect, the instinctual side that reason cannot touch, contains the foolish and sometimes fatal flaw that accounts for the general inability of man to grow or to change. And it is this inability to develop in any meaningful way that makes mankind, in Mary McCarthy's view, essentially comic.

II *Concerning the Comic and Other Matters*

The cold eye that Mary McCarthy casts on the assorted pretensions of man does not prevent her from exploiting what is humorous in the various patterns of his behavior. As noted previously, part of the original contribution of Miss McCarthy is "to have written, from the woman's point of view, the comedy of Sex. The coarse actions are described with an elaborate *verismo* of detail."[3] Brock Brower remarks on her ability to carry off the most scathing critical attack or the most clinical sexual scene "with an uncanny ladylike primness. She would not seem so audacious were she not also so fastidious. Her style, for instance; if there is such a thing as dainty, Ciceronian English, that is what she writes."[4] Obviously, there is no such thing as "dainty Ciceronian English," but Miss McCarthy's style—her voice at once barbarian and aristocratic—does permit her to render the details of sex with an exactingness that can only be described as objective, that is, comic. Sex is not allowed to annihilate the identity of *her* characters. In "Characters in Fiction" she avows that in "making love, we are all more alike than we are when we are talking or acting. . . . The space given to sex in contemporary novels is an avowal of the absence of character. There are no 'people' in *Lady Chatterley's Lover,* unless possibly the husband, who is impotent." And, in writing about sex, she has shown that all that glitters is not gold—that the technology of sex and the incessant talk about sex and the advocacy of sexual freedom sometimes get in the way.

The characters in Mary McCarthy's fiction cerebralize sex as they do everything else. To use D. H. Lawrence's phrase, they have "mentalised" sex by driving it into their brains. Sex is no longer a "dirty little secret" kept underground by the sick gray

Puritans; but the talk and candidness have made sex prosaic. In short, the delight of the secretly shared is missing. Everything having to do with sex has been sterilized and brought out into the open to sun in Central Park like Norine Schmittlapp Blake Rogers' miserable-looking child or confined to a pamphlet in a birth-control bureau. This attitude is another version of Martha Sinnott's saying that if she could not be transparent she did not want to love; if she had to start hiding part of herself from John, then she did not want to remain married to him. The mysterious has no charm in the comic drama of sex, Eastern-Urban style.

Leslie Fiedler has complained in *Love and Death in the American Novel* that no American has yet written a truly great novel depicting heterosexual love that is comparable to *Madame Bovary* or *Anna Karenina*. If anything, Mary McCarthy has set the cause of the heterosexual novel in America back twenty years. For not only does she refuse to celebrate "romantic" love but the picture she does paint of the failure of man and woman to love is extraordinarily grim. Even the "love" affairs that she describes are loveless. Not surprisingly, Miss McCarthy has followed one of the escape routes that traditionally have allowed novelists to avoid the responsibility and demands of writing about heterosexual love. In a sense, *The Company She Keeps, A Charmed Life,* and *The Group* are at least obliquely in the tradition of *The Power of Sympathy* and *Charlotte Temple*— sentimental novels with Margaret Sargent and Martha Sinnott and Kay Petersen the victims of seducers who only play at being husbands. Once again, the American woman is depicted as the long-suffering martyr of love—the inevitable victim of male brutality and lust. Or are men to blame? Are the heroine's freedom and ambition and education the real betrayers? The proper assignation of blame, of course, is not made clear.

Part of the bleakness that Mary McCarthy describes when she focuses on marriage results not only from the limitations inherent in human nature but from the contrariness of dream and fact. The implicit expectations of the heroines are high. In this respect they are victims not only of men but of the myth of "romantic" love. But the concept of romantic love grew out of the courtly love tradition, an extra-marital and literary tradition not meant to survive diapers and mortgage payments and psychoanalysis. Men who are also husbands have been excused their wanderings. Now women who are wives, having a good deal of mobility and leisure time, are in a somewhat analogous situation. Mary McCarthy is too basically honest to gloss over the failure of romantic love pushed into the service of marriage—the occasions when love succumbs to hate or indifference or possessiveness or to the possibility of fulfillment beyond the marriage bed.

III *Concerning Irony and Limitations*

When Mary McCarthy turns away from depicting the comedy of sex to describing the bleakness of marriage and when she abandons topical satire to expose, instead, the general follies of man, she creates characters who fascinate by their irrationality. The lack of confidence that Margaret Sargent exhibits is as "unreasonable" as Mulcahy's paranoia or Martha Sinnott's self-doubt or Kay Petersen's ambition to live through Harald. Yet the illogic that sustains these characters is powerful enough to create a world distinct from that of the satire. But the strength of such fictional personages as Mulcahy or Martha Sinnott acts as an additional agent that dilutes the satirical thrust of these novels. In this light, *The Oasis* is the most successful satire that Miss McCarthy has written because in it she does not let her interest in complexly absorbing characters get the upper hand, although in this work, too, the last word—that of Katy Norell—is ironic. Irony, however, allows Miss McCarthy not only to move beyond satire but to escape any lasting confrontation with the depths of human misery that she has sounded in Mulcahy—a comic villain—or in Martha and Kay—two characters whose mortality removes them from the ranks of the comic, as she has defined that category.

This failing has not escaped Norman Mailer who criticizes Mary McCarthy for choosing "to be not close enough to the horror in the closet. Her nice girls are refugees from the schisms, the wrinklings, and the crater mold of the Upper Middle Class, that radiation belt of well-to-do Protestants full of Church, rectitude, exclusion, guilt, and insanity. . . . Nice girls live on the thin juiceless crust of the horror beneath, the screaming incest, the buried diabolisms of the grand and the would-be-grand. One does not have to have that in one's novel, but one has to have a sense of that madness if the book is to be resonant."[5]

Mary McCarthy does "miss" by having too much furniture in her novels and by not leaving enough space for the play of passions and the drama of growth. But if her concern is satiric and her interest lies in creating characters unaffected by time, then these charges are inconsequential. However, if her purpose is to write not satirical novels but novels that are satiric only peripherally, then the lack of resonance and development that is evident in her fiction becomes a flaw. The chief failure of her fiction to the present is that it commits itself neither to satire nor to the "form" of the novel. The result is a somewhat dichotomous grouping of snatches of brilliant satire and of characters whose complexity involves them in a different—and greater—reality.

IV   *Concerning the Method and Contribution of Mary McCarthy*

Despite these flaws—and even because of some of them—Mary McCarthy has made a significant contribution to American literature. Norman Mailer, who is sensitive to the strengths of Mary McCarthy as well as to her weaknesses, points out that *The Group* possesses one fresh virtue. "It has something new in it; it has a conception of the novel which is Mary's own, a tool by which to cut an ascent into some of the sheer ice faces of the social world. And that is her method. Her Method. For she has divined the first law of our social world, which is that we learn by what we can glean from a hundred alienations of context, from a thousand suffocations of our emotions."[6] And so the cataloguing becomes part not only of the "thingification" of life but a way of depicting man's alienation from himself, from others, from society, and from nature. More than a way of characterizing, the attention paid to the externals and the facts of daily existence provides the bloodless lifeblood of the novels of Mary McCarthy.

The novel has always provided the reader with the sense of his being at the center of the universe. And for this reason, the novel will endure, as Miss McCarthy, even in her most pessimistic moments, affirms. For Mary McCarthy, the proper study has always been man or, more specifically, woman in the society of men and the inanimate "facts" of the everyday. Thus, her subject matter *is* the subject matter of the novel. And it is her voice—speaking out clearly and directly in the essays and drama reviews, becoming modified to fit the demands of the autobiographical heroine or being submerged into the person of Mulcahy or into the persons of "the group" in the fiction, and reappearing again in all its singularity in the travel books—that gives shape to what she sees and conceives. Because she has committed herself so absolutely to the study of man and because she has moved out of a God-centered universe to a man-centered one, the honesty that has become her trademark is also (for want of a larger ethic) her code. "If the flesh must be blind, let the spirit see," Margaret Sargent says in "Ghostly Father, I Confess." Miss McCarthy—one feels—has voiced this same request many times. But because she is a human being, she is not always so honest as she would like to be. Like the rest of us and like her characters, she is a paradox—intelligent, demanding, incorrigible. Unlike most of us, however, Mary McCarthy has the artist's gift of giving form to the paradoxes of existence.

Notes and References

Chapter One

1. Mary McCarthy, *The Company She Keeps* (New York, 1942), Foreword.
2. Elisabeth Niebuhr, "The Art of Fiction XXVII," An Interview with Mary McCarthy, *The Paris Review*, No. 27 (Winter-Spring, 1962), pp. 93-94.
3. Stanley J. Kunitz and Vineta Colby, eds., *Twentieth Century Authors: First Supplement* (New York, 1955), p. 608.
4. Mary McCarthy, *Memories of a Catholic Girlhood* (New York, 1957), p. 10.
5. Kunitz and Colby, *op. cit.*, p. 608.
6. *On the Contrary* (New York, 1962), p. 210. The next six quotations with the exception of that from *Memories of a Catholic Girlhood* are also from "The Vassar Girl." In order to avoid excessive footnoting, page references are included in the text following the quotation.
7. *Ibid.*, p. 99. The next quotation is also from "My Confession."
8. *Partisan Review*, begun by Rahv and Phillips in 1934 as an organ of the John Reed Club of New York, had "died" officially by the fall of 1936. Its editorial policy had differed too sharply from the official Party line. An essay, "In Retrospect," included in *The Partisan Reader: Ten Years of "Partisan Review" 1934-1944: An Anthology*, edited by William Phillips and Philip Rahv (New York, 1946), contains an excellent brief history of this controversial periodical.
9. Kunitz and Colby, *op. cit.*, p. 609.
10. Niebuhr, *op. cit.*, p. 74.
11. *Ibid.*, p. 72.
12. Brock Brower, "Mary McCarthyism," *Esquire*, LVIII (July, 1962), 66. The next two quotations are also from this source.
13. *Letters of James Agee to Father Flye* (New York, 1962), p. 52.
14. *Ibid.*, pp. 52-53.
15. *Mary McCarthy's Theatre Chronicles: 1937-1962* (New York, 1963), p. 207.

Chapter Two

1. *Memories of a Catholic Girlhood*, p. 33. To avoid excessive footnoting, page references from this work are included in the text following the quotation.
2. I have called the individual pieces in *Memories of a Catholic*

Girlhood and "C.Y.E." in *Cast a Cold Eye* "essays." Some amount of arbitrariness may be detected here. And nomenclature may be of little importance. The line that separates the short stories of Mary McCarthy from the essays is admittedly thin. As is shown in the next two chapters, Miss McCarthy herself seems unconcerned about the labels under which her short pieces of writing occur. Generally considered, however, *Memories of a Catholic Girlhood* has as its purpose autobiography and is in the "casual" style of *The New Yorker,* the periodical in which most of these sketches first appeared.

3. "Give a Life to Live," *The Nation,* CLXXXV (July 6, 1957), 17.

4. "The Women and the Orphan Child," *The New Republic,* CXXXVI (June 24, 1957), 19.

5. *A View of My Own: Essays in Literature and Society* (New York, 1963), p. 38.

6. *The Satirist* (Ames, Iowa, 1963), p. 38.

7. Niebuhr, *op. cit.,* p. 64.

8. *Cast a Cold Eye* (New York, 1950), p. 126. I have used as my text the Signet Books edition, first printing September, 1963. Additional page references for quotations from "C.Y.E." appear in the text following the quoted passages and refer to this edition of *Cast a Cold Eye.*

9. Rev. Nelson W. Logal, Review of *Memories of a Catholic Girlhood, The Catholic World,* CLXXXVI (November, 1957), 157.

10. *Ibid.,* p. 158.

11. John W. Simons, "An Author of Few Pieties and Few Illusions," *The Commonweal,* LXVI (July 12, 1957), 380.

Chapter Three

1. Brower, *op. cit.,* p. 62.

2. *Ibid.,* pp. 62, 64.

3. Niebuhr, *op. cit.,* p. 72.

4. *Mary McCarthy's Theatre Chronicles: 1937-1962* (New York, 1963), p. ix. Page numbers to references from *Theatre Chronicles* will be given in parentheses following the particular quotation.

5. New York *Herald Tribune Book Review,* XXXIII, No. 1 (August 23, 1956), 7.

6. *Memories of a Catholic Girlhood,* p. 168.

7. "Mary McCarthy's Vision of Reality," *The New Republic,* CXLV (October 9, 1961), 23.

8. *Ibid.,* p. 24.

9. *On the Contrary: Articles of Belief, 1946-1961* (New York,

1962), p. 57. Page numbers to references from *On the Contrary* will be given in parentheses following the particular quotation.

10. *The New Republic*, October 9, 1961, p. 24.

11. The New York *Times Book Review*, September 24, 1961, p. 6.

Chapter Four

1. Niebuhr, *op. cit.*, p. 71.

2. *Ibid.*, p. 79.

3. *Ibid.*, p. 67.

4. From the "Introduction" to *The Oasis, Horizon*, XIX (February, 1949), n. p.

5. Niebuhr, *op. cit.*, p. 65.

6. Mary McCarthy, *The Company She Keeps* (New York, 1942), p. 30. Page references refer to the Dell Publishing Company, Inc., edition, third Dell printing November, 1957; and these appear subsequently in the text following the quoted passage.

7. Niebuhr, *op. cit.*, p. 65.

8. *Ibid.*, p. 66.

9. "The Novels of Mary McCarthy," *The Creative Present*, edited by Nona Balakian and Charles Simmons (New York, 1963), p. 247.

10. Niebuhr, *op. cit.*, p. 66.

11. "The Novels of Mary McCarthy," *op. cit.*, p. 247.

12. *Ibid.*

13. Mary McCarthy, *Cast a Cold Eye* (New York, 1950), p. 32. Page references are to the Signet Book edition, first printing September, 1963, and appear subsequently in the text following the quoted passage.

14. In a letter written August 15, 1938, to Dorothy Wellesley, William Butler Yeats stated: "I have found a book of essays about Rilke, waiting me, one of Rilkey's [*sic*] ideas about death annoyed me. I wrote on the margin: 'Draw rein; draw breath/Cast a cold eye/On life, on death/Horseman, pass by!'" The last three lines of this quatrain appear in a poem "Under Ben Bulben" which is included in *Last Poems*. This triplet was chosen by Yeats for the epitaph on his tombstone in Drumcliffe churchyard, Sligo.

15. Niebuhr, *op. cit.*, p. 66.

16. *Ibid.*

17. *A View of My Own*, p. 35.

18. *Ibid.*, p. 36.

19. Niebuhr, *op. cit.*, p. 84.

20. *Ibid.*, p. 79.

21. See note #13 of Chapter I.

Chapter Five

1. Gilbert Highet, *The Anatomy of Satire* (Princeton, 1962), p. 3. Page references to additional quotations from this work appear in the text.
2. *On the Contrary*, p. 252.
3. Niebuhr, *op. cit.*, p. 89.
4. *Ibid.*, p. 77.
5. *Ibid.*
6. Contribution to a symposium on "The Cold War and the West," *Partisan Review*, XXIX (Winter, 1962), 50.
7. Brower, *op. cit.*, p. 65.
8. Niebuhr, *op. cit.*, p. 67.
9. *Ibid.*
10. Alex Gottfried and Sue Davidson, "Utopia's Children: An Interpretation of Three Political Novels," *The Western Political Quarterly*, XV (March, 1962), 24.
11. Mary McCarthy, *The Oasis* (New York, 1949), pp. 136-37. Page references are to "The Oasis" as it appears in the Signet edition of *Cast a Cold Eye* and occur in the text following the quoted passage.
12. *On the Contrary*, p. 266.
13. *Cast a Cold Eye*, p. 12.
14. Niebuhr, *op. cit.*, p. 67.
15. Mary McCarthy, *The Groves of Academe* (New York, 1952), pp. 58-59. Page references are to the Signet book edition, first printing October 1963, and appear in the text following the quoted passage.
16. "Characters in Fiction," *On the Contrary*, p. 285.
17. Niebuhr, *op. cit.*, p. 85.
18. *Ibid.*
19. "Characters in Fiction," *On the Contrary*, p. 286.
20. *Ibid.*
21. Kingsley Widmer, "The Academic Comedy," *Partisan Review*, XXVII (Summer, 1960), 526.
22. Louis Auchincloss, *Pioneers & Caretakers, a Study of 9 American Women Novelists* (Minneapolis, 1965), p. 178.

Chapter Six

1. Niebuhr, *op. cit.*, pp. 85-86.
2. *Ibid.*, p. 86.
3. *Ibid.*
4. *Ibid.*

5. *Ibid.,* p. 89.

6. Mary McCarthy, *A Charmed Life* (New York, 1955), p. 12. All additional page references to this work are included in the text following the quoted passage.

7. Niebuhr, *op. cit.,* p. 86.

8. *Ibid.*

9. *Ibid.*

10. *Ibid.*

11. Auchincloss, *op. cit.,* p. 179.

12. *On the Contrary,* p. 252.

13. "Who Is Martha?," *The Nation,* CLXXXI (November 26, 1955), 464.

14. Brower, *op. cit.,* p. 65.

15. *Ibid.,* p. 66.

16. Niebuhr, *op. cit.,* p. 62.

17. *Ibid.,* p. 88.

18. *On the Contrary,* p. 289.

19. Niebuhr, *op. cit.,* p. 62.

20. Mary McCarthy, *The Group* (New York, 1963), p. 360. Additional page references occur in the text following the quoted passage.

21. *On the Contrary,* p. 287.

22. "The Mary McCarthy Case," *The New York Review of Books,* I (October 17, 1963), 3.

23. "My Confession," *On the Contrary,* p. 81.

24. *Ibid.,* p. 83.

25. Niebuhr, *op. cit.,* p. 62.

26. Brower, *op. cit.,* p. 65.

27. "The Mary McCarthy Case," *op. cit.,* p. 2.

28. Letter to the Editor, *Vassar Alumnae Magazine,* XLIX (April, 1964), 64.

29. Letter to the Editor, *Vassar Alumnae Magazine,* XLIX (February, 1964), 32.

30. Niebuhr, *op. cit.,* p. 83.

31. "The Mary McCarthy Case," *op. cit.,* p. 3.

32. *Ibid.*

33. Niebuhr, *op. cit.,* p. 90.

Chapter Seven

1. Mary McCarthy, *Cast a Cold Eye,* p. 58.

2. Niebuhr, *op. cit.,* p. 91.

3. *Ibid.*

4. Mary McCarthy, *The Stones of Florence* (New York, 1959),

p. 4. Additional page references to this work occur in the text following the quoted passage.

5. Mary McCarthy, *Venice Observed* (New York, 1956), p. 6. Additional page references to this work occur in the text following the quoted passage.

6. Niebuhr, *op. cit.,* p. 92.

7. *Ibid.,* p. 93.

8. "Feeling One's Way in Florence," *Times Literary Supplement,* November 13, 1959, p. 662.

Chapter Eight

1. *Theatre Chronicles,* p. 178.

2. *The Oasis,* p. 211.

3. Hardwick, *op. cit.,* p. 36.

4. Brower, *op. cit.,* p. 64.

5. "The Mary McCarthy Case," *The New York Review of Books,* I (October 17, 1963), 3.

6. *Ibid.*

Selected Bibliography

PRIMARY SOURCES

The Company She Keeps. New York: Simon and Schuster, Inc., 1942. Page references in the text are to the Dell Publishing Company, Inc. edition, 3rd. printing November, 1957.

The Oasis. New York: Random House, 1949. This work appears also in *Horizon*, edited by Cyril Connolly. XIX (February, 1949). Page references in the text are to the Signet edition, first printing September, 1963, of *Cast a Cold Eye* in which *The Oasis* also appears.

Cast a Cold Eye. New York: Harcourt, Brace and World, Inc., 1950. Page references in the text are to the Signet edition, first printing September, 1963.

The Groves of Academe. New York: Harcourt, Brace and World, Inc., 1952. Page references in the text are to the Signet edition, first printing October, 1963.

A Charmed Life. New York: Harcourt, Brace and World, Inc., 1955.

Sights and Spectacles: 1937-1956. New York: Farrar, Straus and Company, 1956.

Venice Observed. New York: Reynal and Company, Inc., 1956.

Memories of a Catholic Girlhood. New York: Harcourt, Brace and World, Inc., 1957.

The Stones of Florence. New York: Harcourt, Brace and World, Inc., 1959.

On the Contrary: Articles of Belief, 1946-1961. New York: Noonday Press, 1962.

Mary McCarthy's Theatre Chronicles, 1937-1962. New York: Noonday Press, 1963.

The Group. New York: Harcourt, Brace and World, Inc., 1963.

SECONDARY SOURCES

Note: With one exception, book reviews are not included in the bibliography. Those reviews that are mentioned in the text are cited (with full documentation) in the notes.

BROWER, BROCK. "Mary McCarthyism," *Esquire*, LVIII (July, 1962), 62-67, 113. Interesting for its insights into Miss McCarthy as a person.

CHAMBERLAIN, JOHN. "The Novels of Mary McCarthy," *The Creative Present*. Edited by NONA BALAKIAN and CHARLES SIMMONS. New York: Doubleday and Company, Inc., 1963. The author goes to great lengths to prove that Miss McCarthy is not a political writer and is not serious politically. Of minimal validity because of this bias.

HARDWICK, ELIZABETH. "Mary McCarthy," *A View of My Own: Essays in Literature and Society*. New York: Noonday Press, 1963. An excellent brief appraisal of Miss McCarthy as a writer and as a person.

GOTTFRIED, ALEX, and SUE DAVIDSON. "Utopia's Children: An Interpretation of Three Political Novels," *The Western Political Quarterly*, XV (March, 1962), 17-32. Attempts to link *The Oasis* with Nathaniel Hawthorne's *The Blithedale Romance* and Harvey Swados's *False Coin*. Brings out that these works are novels of utopian ideas (their interest being primarily in the men and women who see the vision and not in the political theory or scheme itself) rather than utopian novels. A good analysis of *The Oasis*.

MAILER, NORMAN. "The Mary McCarthy Case," *The New York Review of Books*, I (October 17, 1963), 1-3. A review of *The Group*, but an excellent one that takes into consideration (although by inference) the totality of Miss McCarthy's writing.

NIEBUHR, ELISABETH. "The Art of Fiction XXVII," *The Paris Review*, XXVII (Winter-Spring, 1962), 58-94. An interview with Miss McCarthy. Extremely helpful in contributing to an understanding of Miss McCarthy's fiction.

Index

Agee, James, 24-25, 97

Bergson, Henri, 73
Bernier, Georges and Rosamond, 156
Broadwater, Bowden, 23-24

Chamberlain, John, 49, 81-82
Charlotte Temple, 177
Chastel, André, 157

Dante, 166-67
De Beauvoir, Simone, 59-60, 62
Dickens, Charles, 19, 62, 68-69, 74, 77

Eliot, T. S., 49

Fiedler, Leslie, 177

Gulliver's Travels, 62, 151

Hiroshima, 56, 60, 173
Hofer, Evelyn, 158
Horace, 173

Johnsrud, Harold, 21-22, 48, 136-37
Juvenal, 21, 173

Lawrence, D. H., 176
Lewis, Wyndham, 174

McCarthy, Mary: family and childhood of, 17-20; education of, 19-21; Vassar College, 20-21, 24, 48, 51, 76, 100, 135-37, 152; facility with Latin, 19-20, 42, 94-95; Catholicism, 18-21, 29-30, 35-36, 38, 40, 47; affiliation with *Partisan Review,* 22-23, 48-52; prose style of, 24, 94-95, 176; use of satire, 29, 100-4, 112-14, 119-24, 135, 152-54, 173-76, 178-79; concept of reflexivity in the writing of, 101-3, 112, 120-22, 152-53, 174-75; use of distortion and exaggeration, 24, 71, 101, 103, 111, 113-14, 123-24, 173-74; use of externals or "facts," 69, 71, 78, 101, 151-53, 174, 179; use of irony, 32, 92, 98-99, 103, 119-20, 122, 132, 136, 153-54, 178; paradox as premise and "solution," 25, 61, 80, 97-99, 101, 138, 150-51, 153-54, 156, 159, 172, 180; characterization in the fiction of, 76-78, 100, 111-12, 120, 122, 135-37, 154, 172, 178; theory concerning the nature and function of comic characters, 73-74, 77-78, 99, 135-36; comic in the writing of, 25, 44, 92, 172, 176; use of a "group" as collective protagonist, 79, 100, 104, 106, 134-35, 171; advantages and limitations of the autobiographical form, 27-28, 43, 47; device of narrative mimicry, 28, 72, 74, 102, 114, 119, 123, 136, 138, 151, 156-57, 175; principle of the author's voice, 28, 72-73, 95, 102, 136, 175, 179-80; bleakness in the writing of, 25, 46-47, 79, 83, 95-98, 103, 126, 177-78; importance of truthfulness in the life and writing of, 47, 49, 56-57, 75, 94, 96-97, 101, 128, 164, 170, 173, 180; self-consciousness in the life and writing of, 37-40, 75, 88, 90-92; theories concerning the craft of fiction, 67, 95; theory concerning the differences between natural and literary symbols, 64-67; achievement of, 179-80

73181

Index